Boston Red Sox IQ:
The Ultimate Test of True Fandom

Bill Nowlin

Printed in the United States of America

Copyright © 2009 by Bill Nowlin

IQ Series books are the trademark of Black Mesa Publishing, LLC.

Cataloging-in-Publication Data is available from the Library of Congress.

ISBN: 144955136X
First edition, first printing

Cover photo by Bill Nowlin.

Black Mesa Publishing, LLC
Florida
David Horne and Marc CB Maxwell
Black.Mesa.Publishing@gmail.com

Contents

Introduction

THINK YOU KNOW RED SOX BASEBALL? Think again. It's time to find out how smart you really are about the Boston Red Sox. Are you a rookie? Are you a tested, hardcore veteran? Or will you be clearing waivers for your pending release halfway through the book?

We'll let you know.

Test your skills. Wrack your brain. It's the ultimate Boston Red Sox IQ test.

Five chapters, more than 250 questions – that's what you're up against, and we're keeping score.

Think of chapter one as Spring Training, that magical time of year when everything just feels so right with the world . . . and, when everybody, even the veterans, gets back to the basics. That's what you will find in the first chapter – questions every Red Sox fan should know, divided among ten different categories:

- The Numbers Game
- The Rookies
- The Veterans
- The Legends
- The Hitters
- The Pitchers
- The Managers, Coaches, Announcers, and Trades
- The Fabulous Feats
- The Teams
- Miscellaneous

In chapter two the season is underway and you're expected to be in shape and ready to play, so be sure and fine tune your mad trivia skills in the first chapter, because when the big club breaks camp the last thing you want is to be left behind with the rookies. The categories are the same but the questions are tougher, and the standings count.

In chapter three find out if you make the All-Star team. You have to start the season strong and then maintain a high level of consistency if you want to be on our All-Star team – and chapter three will toss the wannabes like chaff in the wind.

In chapter four it's the Dog Days of August. Can you make a push for the postseason or are you going to succumb to the pressure, unable to close the deal? We amp it up even more, and when the dust settles we'll let you know if you're deserving of chapter five.

You have to earn your way to chapter five. This is the postseason. This is where you will find trivia befitting a world champion. This is where legends are made. This is your Red Sox IQ, the Ultimate Test of True Fandom.

Chapter One

SPRING TRAINING

THIS IS SPRING TRAINING mind you. We're only stretching here. Just trying to get limber after a long winter of chips, couches, remote controls, beverages of choice, and the NFL . . . I mean, there's no sense straining a groin or anything else right out of the box. So we'll just start with some basics – a few Red Sox legends and some numbers that go with them.

(Babe Ruth. Courtesy of the Boston Red Sox)

No point in sweating bullets over these questions. You don't know these, well, you don't know jack.

THE NUMBERS GAME

QUESTION 1: He's got the Pesky Pole named after him. How many home runs did Johnny Pesky hit for the Red Sox?
   a) 13
   b) 35
   c) 66
   d) 104

QUESTION 2: Why did every player on the Red Sox wear the same number on one day in 2009, and what number was it?

QUESTION 3: What number did Babe Ruth wear when he was a member of the Red Sox?

QUESTION 4: What's the longest winning streak for any Red Sox team?

QUESTION 5: What Boston batter was hit by pitches 35 times in 1986, setting an American League record?

THE ROOKIES

QUESTION 6: Who were the "Gold Dust Twins"?

QUESTION 7: When given the opportunity, to which award-winning ballplayer did the Red Sox decline to offer a contract?
   a) 1947 Rookie of the Year Jackie Robinson
   b) 1950 Rookie of the Year Sam Jethroe
   c) 1951 Rookie of the Year Willie Mays
   d) All of the above

QUESTION 8: A number of Red Sox players, from Marty McHale ("the Irish Thrush") to Maury McDermott, have been noted singers on stage in theaters and nightclubs. Who was the most noted as a recording artist?

QUESTION 9: What were the circumstances that led to the Standells song "Love That Dirty Water" becoming the victory anthem of the Boston Red Sox?

QUESTION 10: What was perhaps an even-better come-from-behind victory?

THE VETERANS

QUESTION 11: There was one Red Sox player who appeared in more than a dozen Opening Day games and recorded a hit in every one of them. Who was it?

QUESTION 12: What Red Sox player was a teammate with Ted Williams, Hank Aaron, Bill Russell, and Bob Cousy?

QUESTION 13: There was another man who played for the Red Sox, the Celtics, *and* the Bruins. Who was he?

QUESTION 14: Carl Yastrzemski played in the most Red Sox games ever (3,308). Who's in second place?
    a) Cy Young
    b) Harry Hooper
    c) Joe Cronin
    d) Ted Williams
    e) Dwight Evans

QUESTION 15: What Red Sox hitter banged a home run off both a father and his son?

THE LEGENDS

QUESTION 16: Who played for the Red Sox in parts of four different decades?

QUESTION 17: Nuf Ced McGreevy was effectively the leader of the Royal Rooters, an early 20th century booster club. Why was McGreevy's barroom named the "Third Base Saloon"?

QUESTION 18: What's the story about the song "Tessie"?

QUESTION 19: What Red Sox player served in the same U. S. Marine Corps squadron as John Glenn during the Korean War, sometimes flying as Glenn's wingman?

QUESTION 20: Who did no less than Ted Williams dub "the silent captain" of the Boston Red Sox?

THE HITTERS

QUESTION 21: Only two sluggers have hit 50 or more home runs in a single season for the Red Sox. Who are they?

QUESTION 22: What player hit three home runs on his birthday?

QUESTION 23: Which Red Sox player has the most RBIs in postseason play?

QUESTION **24:** Who has hit the most homers in the postseason for the Red Sox?

QUESTION **25:** Which player made the word "taters" well-known in Red Sox lore?

THE PITCHERS

QUESTION **26:** This player had twice as many homers as anyone else on the team, and was second as a pitcher in wins – but his manager elected to use him just once, as a pinch-hitter, in the World Series. Who was he, and why wasn't he used more?

QUESTION **27:** What pitcher recorded the most strikeouts in one inning, tying a major league record?

QUESTION **28:** Which Red Sox pitcher led the league in saves one year, then threw a no-hitter a little over 18 months later?

QUESTION **29:** Who holds the Red Sox record for the most strikeouts in one season?

QUESTION **30:** Which Red Sox pitcher won 16 games in a row, establishing a major league record?

THE MANAGERS, COACHES, ANNOUNCERS, AND TRADES

QUESTION **31:** Who did the Red Sox get from the Expos for three-time 17-game winner Bill Lee (94-68 with the Red Sox)?

QUESTION 32: Who did the Red Sox get from Seattle for relief pitcher Heathcliff Slocumb (5-10 with Boston)?

QUESTION 33: Who did the Sox get from the Yankees for future Cy Young Award-winning reliever Sparky Lyle?

QUESTION 34: Taters & cheese? Speaking of food slang, who was the player (and later announcer) who introduced "cheese" as a term indicating a good pitch?

QUESTION 35: What four words uttered by Joe Castiglione are four of the happiest words most Red Sox fans of today bear in their memory?

BONUS QUESTION: So Foulke underhanded the ball to first, but what happened to that final ball when the Sox won their first world championship in 86 years?

THE FABULOUS FEATS

QUESTION 36: In 1975, when Fisk waved his home run fair in Game Six, what inning was it?

QUESTION 37: Whose 1975 World Series home run was arguably more important than Carlton Fisk's famous extra-inning homer in Game Six?

QUESTION 38: What was the "bloody sock" and what two unexpected contributors played such a key role in Red Sox postseason history?

QUESTION 39: Have there ever been two triple plays in one game?

QUESTION 40: Who has the best postseason record of any pitcher in baseball history?
   a) Babe Ruth
   b) Dave Ferriss
   c) Pedro Martinez
   d) Curt Schilling

THE TEAMS

QUESTION 41: Why was the "Impossible Dream" of 1967 so improbable?

QUESTION 42: Speaking of losing streaks, when the Impossible Dream team won the pennant in 1967, they'd suffered through how many consecutive losing seasons?

QUESTION 43: Twice, the Red Sox had the chance to win a single-game playoff and win the American League pennant. Name the years and their opponents.

QUESTION 44: When did a New York electronic message board flash the words "Congratulations, World Champion Boston Red Sox"?

QUESTION 45: Can it really be true that one pitcher won the deciding game of all three stages of the 2004 postseason?

MISCELLANEOUS

QUESTION 46: What could be more important in Boston than the inaugural game of a new ballpark? Opening Day any year is always huge news, but why was coverage of the very first game ever at brand-new Fenway Park not featured more in the Boston media?

QUESTION 47: Who wrote that Fenway Park was "a lyric little bandbox of a park"?

QUESTION 48: Why is one seat in the Fenway Park bleachers a different color (red) from the others, which are green?

QUESTION 49: What umpire had to travel with FBI protection after his controversial ruling in a World Series game?

QUESTION 50: What Boston ballplayer insisted the team assess him the maximum-allowable 28% pay cut?

Chapter One Answer Key

Time to find out how you did – put a check mark next to the questions you answered correctly, and when you are done be sure and add up your score to find out your IQ, and to find out if you made the Opening Day roster.

THE NUMBERS GAME

___ **QUESTION 1:** A – The correct answer is 13. He hit a total of 17 in his big-league career.

___ **QUESTION 2:** The number was 42, and on Jackie Robinson Day in 2009, every umpire, coach, manager, and player throughout baseball wore #42. This led to some amusing visuals as #42 scooped the ball and fired to #42, beating #42 at first base by a step, as coach #42 looked on and umpire #42 signaled, "Out!"

___ **QUESTION 3:** None. The Red Sox first wore numbers in 1931, and The Babe was long gone from Boston.

___ **QUESTION 4:** The best streak for the Red Sox was 15 straight wins in 1946, from April 25 to May 10.

___ **QUESTION 5:** Don Baylor, who also held the modern major league record until dethroned by Houston's black-and-blue Craig Biggio, 285-267.

THE ROOKIES

___ **QUESTION 6:** Fred Lynn and Jim Rice, dubbed as such in their 1975 rookie seasons.

___ QUESTION 7: The three named players also accounted for three MVP awards – two for Mays and one for Robinson. In each case, the Red Sox had the unencumbered opportunity to sign the player as a pure free agent. Needless to say, there are numerous other African American players they could have signed as well. The answer to the question, sadly, is D – All of the above, and it's difficult to doubt that racism hadn't cost the Red Sox a pennant or two.

___ QUESTION 8: Tony Conigliaro.

___ QUESTION 9: It was Opening Day in 1998, and the Red Sox were losing to Seattle, 7-2, heading into the bottom of the ninth. One can be sure that more than a few people had already made their way out of the ballpark. The Red Sox rallied, with Mo Vaughn's grand slam walk-off creating a miraculous come-from-behind victory. Sound man Kevin Friend was waiting for a moment like this, and one second after the homer hit, he put the song on the Fenway Park sound system and it blared out to the thousands who remained: "Aw-oh, Boston, you're my home!"

___ QUESTION 10: On June 18, 1961, what has to be one of the greatest games in Red Sox history (plug: to learn more about it, read *The 50 Greatest Red Sox Games*) saw the Sox down by seven runs in the bottom of the ninth, in part because Willie Tasby had hit a grand slam for the Senators in the top of the ninth. Boston was losing 12-5, with two outs and one man on. They won the game. They scored three runs, and then Jim Pagliaroni hit a grand slam to tie the game. Bases cleared, the Sox started populating them once more with a Wertz walk, a

Buddin single, and a pinch-hit walk-off from Russ Nixon. And then the Sox won the second game that day, 6-5, in 13 innings.

THE VETERANS

___ **QUESTION 11:** Ted Williams hit safely in every one of the 14 Opening Day games in which he appeared.

___ **QUESTION 12:** Sox pitcher Gene Conley also played pro sports as a center for the Boston Celtics of the NBA, serving as Bill Russell's backup on the 1959, 1960, and 1961 World Champion Boston Celtics. Because he'd also been on the 1957 World Champion Milwaukee Braves, Conley remains the only professional sports player on champion teams in two sports. As it happens, he also won the 1955 All-Star Game (in baseball). Conley had played for the Boston Braves before the team relocated to Milwaukee, thus making him also the only pro to play for three professional teams from the same city – Braves, Red Sox, and Celtics.

___ **QUESTION 13:** Organist John Kiley.

___ **QUESTION 14:** E – It's Evans, with 2,505.

___ **QUESTION 15:** Ted Williams, who hit one off Thornton Lee in 1940, and Don Lee in 1960.

THE LEGENDS

___ **QUESTION 16:** Ted Williams, 1939-60. And he's the only one.

___ QUESTION 17: The answer was provided in its slogan: "the last stop before you go home."

___ QUESTION 18: In the 1903 World Series, the Boston Americans were scuffling. They needed something of a spark. The Royal Rooters contingent which had taken the train to Pittsburg bought sheet music of a popular song of the day, "Tessie," and fashioned new lyrics to it, such as one making fun of the Pirates' Honus Wagner ("Honus, why do you hit so badly?"), and hired a band which played it incessantly – ten or more times in a row. Sophomoric as it may have been, the endless rendering of the song would get on anyone's nerves. Soon afterward, the tide turned in Boston's favor and they went on to win the Series. For years, "Tessie" was played at all key Boston ballgames. Even decades later, Pittsburgh's third baseman Tommy Leach said, 'I think those Boston fans won the Series . . . We beat them three out of four games, and then they started singing that damn Tessie song . . . Sort of got on your nerves after a while. And before we knew what happened, we'd lost the Series.'" [*Love That Dirty Water*] In 2004, Dr. Charles Steinberg of the Red Sox worked with Jeff Horrigan of the *Boston Herald* and Ken Casey of the Dropkick Murphys band and developed a new version of "Tessie." The first time they played the song live at Fenway, the Sox fashioned a spectacular comeback against the Yankees, and ultimately went on to win that year's World Series. Ever since, if the Red Sox win the game – any game – the first song that plays in the park is "Love That Dirty Water" followed immediately by "Tessie." It's tradition.

___ QUESTION 19: Capt. Theodore Samuel Williams.

___ **QUESTION 20:** Bobby Doerr.

THE HITTERS

___ **QUESTION 21:** Jimmie Foxx hit exactly 50 in 1938. David Ortiz hit 54 in 2006. Foxx was a right-handed hitter; Ortiz hit lefty. Foxx played in a 154-game season, Ortiz when the season was 162 games long.

___ **QUESTION 22:** On July 23, 2002, the Tampa Bay pitching staff gave Nomar Garciaparra three gifts for his 29th birthday in the form of two two-run homers in a ten-run third inning (off Sturtze and Backe) and a third blast in the fourth (again off Backe).

___ **QUESTION 23:** David Ortiz, who has 43 through the 2009 postseason.

___ **QUESTION 24:** No surprise – also Big Papi David Ortiz, with 13.

___ **QUESTION 25:** George "The Boomer" Scott called his home runs taters.

THE PITCHERS

___ **QUESTION 26:** Babe Ruth, despite an 18-8 record during the 1915 season and an earned run average of 2.44, never took part in the 1915 World Series other than to pinch-hit for Ernie Shore in the ninth inning of Game One. He grounded out. During the regular season, Ruth led the Red Sox in home runs (with four) and was ninth in the league. As a pitcher, he was second in the league in hits allowed per nine innings pitched, and fourth in the league in winning percentage – but manager Bill Carrigan chose not to use him in the World Series. For years there were stories that Carrigan was showing Ruth who was boss, a disciplinary matter. Leigh Montville reports in *The Big Bam* that Carrigan explained later that "he never pitched Ruth because he simply had other, better pitchers at the time."

___ **QUESTION 27:** Tim Wakefield struck out four batters in the bottom of the ninth inning in a game in Kansas City on August 10, 1999. It was a potentially costly passed ball charged to Jason Varitek. The score was in Boston's favor, 5-3. The first two batters in the inning had whiffed, and Wakefield struck out the Royals' Johnny Damon. Had Tek held the ball, the game would have been over. Instead, Damon scampered to first base, and then scored on Carlos Febles' game-tying two-run homer. Wake then struck out Carlos Beltran to end the inning. The game continued, the Sox scoring four times in the top of the tenth. Wakefield got a couple of outs, gave up a couple of doubles, then struck out Chad Kreuter for the final out of the game – except that, once more, there was a passed ball and the runner reached first base. In came reliever Rich Garces, who struck out the one batter he faced, this time truly ending the game.

___ **QUESTION 28:** Derek Lowe led the league in saves in 2000, and then threw a no-hitter on April 27, 2002.

___ **QUESTION 29:** Pedro Martinez struck out 313 opponents in 1999, by far the most Ks recorded in a single season by a Red Sox pitcher. Roger Clemens ranks second with 291 (1988).

___ **QUESTION 30:** The longest streak of consecutive victories by a Red Sox pitcher came in 1912 when Smoky Joe Wood won 16 in a row. After a 4-3 loss to Philadelphia on the Fourth of July, Wood won 16 in a row beginning with a 5-1 win over St. Louis. He beat the Browns, then Detroit, Chicago, Cleveland, Chicago, St. Louis, Cleveland, Detroit, St. Louis, Detroit, Cleveland, Chicago, New York, Washington, Chicago, and St. Louis. There were six shutouts in the streak, and over the 16 games Wood yielded just 27 runs.

THE MANAGERS, COACHES, ANNOUNCERS, AND TRADES

___ **QUESTION 31:** Stan Papi, who hit .188 for the Red Sox.

___ **QUESTION 32:** Both Derek Lowe and Jason Varitek.

___ **QUESTION 33:** Danny Cater, who hit a serviceable .262 over three seasons, and Mario Guerrero, who hit .241 over two.

___ **QUESTION 34:** Dennis Eckersley, who's been known to say things while broadcasting such as, "That was big-league cheese. It had some hair on it."

___ **QUESTION 35:** "Can you believe it?" His full call of the final play of the 2004 World Series will never tire: "Swing and a ground ball, stabbed by Foulke. He has it. He underhands to first, and the Boston Red Sox are the world champions! For the first time in 86 years, the Red Sox have won baseball's world championship. Can you believe it?" In this day and age, probably more fans were watching on television than listening on radio (though some still turn down the audio on national broadcasts in favor of listening to local broadcasters), but virtually no one remembers what whoever was broadcasting the national TV feed had to say. It's the local call that lives on in fame.

BONUS QUESTION: Somehow first baseman Doug Mientkiewicz had the presence of mind to hold onto it. Doing so, however, caused a controversy which raged on for a few months – despite a long-standing tradition of players keeping key balls (their first base hit, the game ball from a big win, etc.), there were many who felt such an historic ball should be the property of the Red Sox. In the end, after almost 18 months, a compromise of some sort was reached through arbitration and the ball had a permanent home at the Hall of Fame.

THE FABULOUS FEATS

___ **QUESTION 36:** It was the bottom of the 12th inning, and Fisk was the first man up.

___ **QUESTION 37:** Bernie Carbo's – he came up as a pinch-hitter in the bottom of the eighth inning with two outs and two on, and the Red Sox losing by three runs, facing elimination. He banged a game-tying homer into the center-field seats. Without Carbo's homer, Fisk's might well never have happened.

___ **QUESTION 38:** The sock itself wasn't important. It was the man who wore it who was, and what Curt Schilling brought to the 2004 postseason. Schilling had led the league with 21 wins (21-6) during the regular season, and won his game against Anaheim in the Division Series. He'd hurt his ankle, though, and was uncertain against the Yankees in the ALCS. He tried, starting Game One, but had to leave in serious pain after three innings and six runs. Enter team doctor Bill Morgan who envisioned a way to "sew in place" the tendons in Schilling's right ankle as a temporary fix. Contributor #2 was an unnamed cadaver on which Morgan experimented, after Curt agreed to give it a try. Come Game Six, with the Sox still unexpectedly in contention despite having lost the first three games in the best-of-seven set, Schilling threw six shutout innings and allowed just one run in the seventh, sufficiently silencing the Yanks – all while TV viewers could plainly see a small red stain on his ankle as blood seeped out from around the site of the suturing that Dr. Morgan had performed. In the World Series, Schilling threw six more innings against St. Louis in Game Two, allowing only one unearned run.

___ **QUESTION 39:** Yes, the Twins pulled off identical 5-4-3 triple plays in the fifth and eighth innings vs. Boston on July 17, 1990, but Boston won the game, 1-0. The next day, the Sox hit into six double plays, while turning four themselves. The ten DPs in one game set a record of its own. Boston won that game, 5-4.

___ **QUESTION 40:** D – Curt Schilling, who was 11-2 in the postseason. For the Phillies, he was 1-1, for the Diamondbacks, he was 4-0, and for the Red Sox he was 6-1.

THE TEAMS

___ **QUESTION 41:** In 1966, in a ten-team league, the Red Sox had finished in ninth place, just half a game ahead of the last-place team: the New York Yankees.

___ **QUESTION 42:** Eight!

___ **QUESTION 43:** Cleveland Indians (1948) and New York Yankees (1978).

___ **QUESTION 44:** More than 20 years later, it's still painful to remember 1986. Late in Game Six at Shea Stadium, a New York Mets employee prematurely flashed those words in preparation for it becoming a reality. The Red Sox were up three games to two, heading into Game Six. It looked like it was all over, after the Red Sox took a 5-3 lead in the top of the tenth, and the first two Mets batters went down routinely. The message flashed. The champagne was ready in the clubhouse. The plastic drapes were up to protect the players' clothing from the spraying champagne that is *de rigeur* after playoff series wins. Then things changed.

___ **QUESTION 45:** Yes, it is true. Derek Lowe came on in relief in Game Three of the Division Series, and pitched the top of the tenth inning of a 6-6 game against the Angels. That's all he needed to get the win, when David Ortiz hit a two-run homer in the bottom of the tenth. In the Championship Series, he started Game Four but was long gone when that was resolved (by another Ortiz two-run walk-off home run) in the bottom of the 12th. He did, however, start Game Seven as well, in Yankee Stadium, and left after six innings with an 8-1 lead. The bullpen held that lead. Lowe started Game Four of the World Series, in St. Louis, with the Red Sox having already won the first three games. This time he pitched shutout ball for seven innings (just three hits and one walk) and the three runs the Sox had scored early on held up.

MISCELLANEOUS

___ QUESTION 46: The "media" at the time was only the newspapers. There were quite a few of them in Boston, but the sinking of the steamship HMS Titanic pretty much pushed Fenway off the front pages.

___ QUESTION 47: Pulitzer Prize and National Book Award winner John Updike, in his famous essay in *The New Yorker* on Ted Williams' last game.

___ QUESTION 48: The famous "red seat" is situated in section 42, in row 37 – 502 feet from home plate. Though sluggers like David Ortiz and Manny Ramirez have both expressed disbelief that anyone can hit a baseball that far (both have admitted trying to do so in batting practice and coming nowhere close), it really happened. Ted Williams struck a ball on June 9, 1946, which put a hole in the straw hat worn by one Joseph A. Boucher, who was pictured in the following day's newspaper. At the time, and for many years afterward, there were no actual seats in the bleachers, but merely long boards serving as benches on which patrons sat.

___ QUESTION 49: Larry Barnett, who had ruled that Ed Armbrister was not to be called out for interfering with Carlton Fisk when the Red Sox catcher collided with

Armbrister when trying to field the Cincinnatians' bunt in front of home plate. Barnett received a number of death threats after his ruling, which effectively cost the Red Sox a win, and perhaps the Series.

___ **QUESTION 50:** After his 1959 season, when he only hit .254, nearly .100 points below his career average, Ted Williams wanted to come back for one final year, but insisted that owner Tom Yawkey tear up the contract presented and submit one that was significantly lower.

Got your Spring Training total? Here's how it breaks down:

NO DROP STATUS IN FANTASY LEAGUES EVERYWHERE	= 45-50
OPENING DAY STARTER	= 40-44
YOU MADE IT TO THE SHOW	= 35-39
PLATOON PLAYER AT BEST	= 30-34
ANOTHER SEASON IN THE MINORS	= 00-29

Good luck on Opening Day!

Chapter Two

OPENING DAY

THEY ALL COUNT NOW, no pressure. You made the roster with the big club and now you're looking forward to earning a big contract, some major endorsements perhaps, or being a part of the Sunday Conversation on SportsCenter, but most importantly, you're here to win the big game.

(Mo Vaughn, going deep. Courtesy of the Boston Red Sox)

So game on!

Let's find out how well you can do after we ratchet things up a notch. The categories stay the same, but everything else is more intense. We're about to find out whether or not you can play this game for a living.

THE NUMBERS GAME

QUESTION 51: Which Red Sox batter had the highest batting average in the 2004 World Series?
- a) David Ortiz
- b) Manny Ramirez
- c) Bill Mueller
- d) Johnny Damon

QUESTION 52: Who had the most runs batted in during a single season by a Red Sox batter?

QUESTION 53: What are the most runs the Red Sox scored in a single inning?

QUESTION 54: You read already that Carl Yastrzemski played in a franchise record 3,308 regular season games, but . . . how many games did the Hall of Fame legend get to play in the postseason?

QUESTION 55: Who scored the most runs in one game?

THE ROOKIES

QUESTION 56: What two major league rookie records has Ted Williams held since 1939?

QUESTION 57: What 21-year-old rookie came within one strike of pitching a no-hitter in his very first game, in Yankee Stadium no less?

QUESTION 58: Which Red Sox players hit home runs in their first game at Fenway Park?
    a) Eddie Pellagrini
    b) Butch Hobson
    c) Tony Conigliaro
    d) Wilfred Lefebvre
    e) All of the above

QUESTION 59: Who was the first Rookie of the Year for the Red Sox?

QUESTION 60: In 1956, as a sophomore at the University of Oklahoma, he actually outscored Wilt Chamberlain in a collegiate basketball game – and just five years later, he was the 1961 American League Rookie of the Year. Can you name this Red Sox pitcher?

THE VETERANS

QUESTION 61: What's the name of the veteran pitcher who, when asked to pitch on October 4, 1948, reportedly turned "white as a ghost"?

QUESTION 62: It's said that this Hall of Famer who tripped rounding third base may have cost the Red Sox a pennant. Who was it?

QUESTION 63: Fans remember how Bill Buckner played hard for a few years with bandaged, aching legs. What was remarkable about his very last home run for the Red Sox?

QUESTION 64: What ballplayer has had his number retired by two different ballclubs, the Red Sox and one other?

QUESTION 65: Which Red Sox player who placed second lost the A.L. batting title by the slimmest margin?
   a) Johnny Pesky in 1942 (.331)
   b) Ted Williams in 1949 (.343)
   c) Carl Yastrzemski in 1970 (.329)
   d) Fred Lynn in 1975 (.331)
   e) Wade Boggs in 1991 (.332)

THE LEGENDS

QUESTION 66: Can you name the Red Sox player who was asked to attend a conference in Switzerland, issued a pistol, and given orders to kill German physicist Werner Heisenberg if the player's assessment was that the Nazis were close to developing atomic weaponry?

QUESTION 67: Cy Young won the most games of any Red Sox pitcher, but was he ever a 20-game loser?

QUESTION 68: You may have heard that Wade Boggs once hit .400 over a season's worth of 162 games, but is that just a folk legend?

QUESTION 69: What's one remarkable stat about The Monster? Not the wall, the *pitcher*.

QUESTION 70: Which pitcher (with at least 20 decisions) had the best career record against the New York Yankees?

THE HITTERS

QUESTION 71: What Red Sox player holds the record for the most doubles in a single season?

QUESTION 72: What Red Sox hitter reached base the most times in a row, without an out, and how many times did he reach?

QUESTION 73: Who holds the longest hitting streak in Red Sox history?

QUESTION 74: Who was the first batting champion for the Red Sox?

QUESTION 75: To record 400 total bases in a single season is quite an accomplishment. Who was the last player in the American League to achieve this and when did he do it?

THE PITCHERS

QUESTION 76: True or false: the very first game the Boston Americans ever played was a loss, by a pitcher named Win?

QUESTION 77: Has there ever been a Red Sox pitcher who appeared in at least 50% of a season's games?

QUESTION 78: What Red Sox pitcher still holds the major league record for the lowest earned run average ever recorded?

QUESTION 79: What two Red Sox pitchers won the Pitching Triple Crown?

QUESTION 80: What pitcher allowed the most home runs in any major league game?

THE MANAGERS, COACHES, ANNOUNCERS, AND TRADES

QUESTION 81: What bold prediction did Dick Williams make when assuming the reins of the 1967 Red Sox?

QUESTION 82: How many of Boston's managers have committed suicide during their tenure with the team?

QUESTION 83: What former Red Sox manager was sentenced to four years at hard labor in state prison after pleading guilty to negligent homicide when his car went out of control and killed a highway worker?

QUESTION 84: Which Red Sox batting coach made his big league debut as a member of the 1986 New York Mets? He batted 8-for-18 (.444) during a September call-up, but he was not on the Mets playoff roster that defeated Boston in the World Series.

QUESTION 85: Who was the first manager in franchise history to lead the Red Sox to the postseason three different times?

THE FABULOUS FEATS

QUESTION 86: Which Red Sox players have won the Triple Crown – leading the league in batting average, home runs, and runs batted in all in the same year?

QUESTION 87: Ted Williams homered 521 times for the Red Sox. How many of those home runs were the game-winning hits?
  a) 34
  b) 46
  c) 57
  d) 96

QUESTION 88: Of those 521 homers, how many were inside-the-parkers?

QUESTION 89: What Red Sox hitter had a season when he hit more home runs than strikeouts?

QUESTION 90: Which Red Sox player won the most Gold Gloves?

THE TEAMS

QUESTION 91: What All-Star shortstop tried to negotiate a $25 million pay cut for himself so he could join the Red Sox?

QUESTION 92: Every Patriots Day, the Red Sox start the day's game in the morning. What Boston team made the earliest start ever in franchise history?

QUESTION 93: When Boston won Game Seven of the 1903 World Series and took a 4-games-to-3 lead over Pittsburg, why did the two teams play another game three days later?

QUESTION 94: Who is the only player since World War II to earn World Series rings for both the Red Sox and the Yankees?

QUESTION 95: Which of Boston's world championship teams won the fewest games during the regular season in which it claimed the pennant and went on to win the World Series?

MISCELLANEOUS

QUESTION 96: On May 22, 1984 a Red Sox fielder reached his glove down and scooped up . . . a rodent. Who was the fielder?

QUESTION 97: Is it true that the Yankees once owned Fenway Park?

QUESTION 98: Ted Williams, angry at himself, threw his bat and was horrified when it flew into the stand and hit a woman. Whose housekeeper was she?

QUESTION 99: Other than selling out Fenway Park every home game since May 15, 2003, what (even longer) streak do the Red Sox hold?

QUESTION 100: Who was the person working for the

Red Sox who wrote one of rock & roll's oldies classics, "Summertime, Summertime"?

Chapter Two Answer Key

Time to find out how you did – put a check mark next to the questions you answered correctly, and when you are done be sure and add up your score to find out your IQ, and to find out if you deserve a shot at the Mid-Summer Classic.

THE NUMBERS GAME

___ QUESTION 51: C – Bill Mueller, .429. Manny hit .412, Ortiz .308, and Damon .286.

___ QUESTION 52: Jimmie Foxx, with 175 RBIs in 1938. Second was the Williams/Stephens combo in 1949 – 159 RBIs apiece – a quick calculation shows a total of 318 combined. David Ortiz comes next, with his 148 in 2005. The highest total not to win the RBI crown was the 144 Manny Ramirez drove in that same year, 2005 – because Ortiz drove in four more. Foxx had over 100 at Fenway Park alone! (104).

___ QUESTION 53: The largest amounts of runs scored by the Red Sox in single innings were the 17 runs scored by the Red Sox on June 18, 1953 and the 14 runs scored in the very first inning of the June 27, 2003 ballgame against the team that became that year's World Champions, the Florida Marlins.

___ QUESTION 54: Yaz is second in baseball history for career regular season games but he played only 17 in the postseason. Boston won pennants with Yaz in 1967 and 1975 but lost the World Series in seven games both times. His other three postseason games came during the 1975 LCS.

___ **QUESTION 55:** The major league record is shared by two Red Sox: six runs. Johnny Pesky did this on May 8, 1946, and Spike Owen did it 40 years later, on August 21, 1986.

THE ROOKIES

___ **QUESTION 56:** Walks (107) and RBIs (145).

___ **QUESTION 57:** Billy Rohr, on April 14, 1967, sustained a no-hitter against the Yankees for 8 2/3 innings. Yankees catcher Elston Howard singled to right-center field to spoil the no-no, but Rohr still has himself a superb 3-0 one-hit shutout against Whitey Ford. Reggie Smith's leadoff homer was the only run truly needed in the game.

___ **QUESTION 58:** E – All of the above. Hobson was perhaps the most unusual one in that it happened so much later than his actual debut. He'd appeared in two road games in 1975, but Butch marked his June 28, 1976 Fenway Park debut with a double off the center-field wall and an inside-the-park home run, helping the Sox win, 12-8, over Baltimore.

___ **QUESTION 59:** Walt Dropo, 1950. The 144 runs he drove in that year had an awful lot to do with it.

___ **QUESTION 60:** Don Schwall, despite the fact he actually started 1961 in the minors. Not only that, he didn't make his big league debut until May 21, and yet he still made the

All-Star team! He finished the season a very impressive 15-7 in only 25 starts.

THE VETERANS

___ **QUESTION 61:** That would be Denny Galehouse, manager Joe McCarthy's surprise choice to pitch the single-game playoff against the Cleveland Indians that would determine which team won the American League pennant. Galehouse's won-loss record was 8-7 at the time, and he lost the game, 8-3.

___ **QUESTION 62:** Luis Aparicio in 1972, when Boston missed out, falling a half-game short.

___ **QUESTION 63:** It was an inside-the-park home run – hit by perhaps the last man you'd think could leg it around the bases before the ball was thrown home. At Fenway Park on April 25, 1990, the 41-year-old player hit a drive off Kirk McCaskill of the Angels. It was a drive to right, and Claudell Washington crashed into the stands, hurting his knee so badly he later had to leave the game. The *Globe's* Frank Dell'Apa wrote that it was "likely the first homer in which the ball remained in play and the fielder went over the fence."

___ **QUESTION 64:** Catcher Carlton Fisk had his number 27 retired by the Red Sox in September 2000; his number 72 had already been retired by the White Sox in September 1997. (Nolan Ryan's number was retired by three teams, but he never played for the Red Sox.)

___ **QUESTION 65:** B – the mathematically correct answer is Ted Williams. In 1949, George Kell was .3429118 and

Williams was .3427561, for a difference of just .0001557. In 1942, Pesky's .331 was second only to Ted Williams (.356) but was second by .025 points. In 1970, Alex Johnson hit .3289902 and Yaz hit .3286219, a difference of .0003683. In 1975, Rod Carew beat Lynn handily, .359 to .331. In 1991, Julio Franco's .342 was .009 points above Boggs.

THE LEGENDS

___ **QUESTION 66:** Moe Berg, catcher for the Red Sox from 1935-39, under assignment from U. S. intelligence during World War II.

___ **QUESTION 67:** In 1906, despite a decent 3.19 ERA, Cy Young was a 20-game loser with a record of 13-21.

___ **QUESTION 68:** It's actually true. Wade Boggs actually hit over .400 for a 162-game stretch; it was just his historic misfortune that he didn't do it within one calendar year. From June 13, 1985 through June 8, 1986, Boggs hit over .400.

___ **QUESTION 69:** Dick Radatz won 15 games in 1963 and 16 games in 1964 – as a relief pitcher. In '63, only Bill Monbouqette won more (20-10), but Radatz had a 1.97 ERA compared to Monbo's 3.81. In 1964, he had more wins than any pitcher on the staff. Monbo was second, with 13 wins.

___ **QUESTION 70:** Babe Ruth, who was 17-5.

THE HITTERS

___ **QUESTION 71:** Earl Webb, 67 (1931) – for nearly 80 years now, still the major league record.

___ **QUESTION 72:** In 1957, soon after he turned 39, Williams reached base in a record 16 consecutive plate appearances:

Sept. 17 vs. KC – pinch-hit home run
Sept. 18 vs. KC – pinch-hit walk
Sept. 20 at NY – pinch-hit home run
Sept. 21 at NY – home run, three walks
Sept. 22 at NY – home run, single, two walks
Sept. 23 at NY – single, three walks, hit by pitch

As noted by SABR's Cliff Otto, this string includes four home runs in four consecutive official at-bats.

___ **QUESTION 73:** It was set in 1949 by Dominic DiMaggio, hitting in 34 consecutive games. You may have heard - his brother Joe holds the major league mark.

___ **QUESTION 74:** Dale Alexander, 1932.

___ **QUESTION 75:** Jim Rice, 1978: 406 total bases.

THE PITCHERS

___ **QUESTION 76:** True. The first franchise game was played on April 26, 1901. The starting pitchers were "Iron Man" Joe McGinnity (Baltimore Orioles) and Win Kellum (Boston Americans). Baltimore won, 10-6.

___ **QUESTION 77:** Yes, once. Mike Timlin appeared in exactly 81 games in 2005, half of the 162-game schedule.

___ **QUESTION 78:** Dutch Leonard's 0.96 ERA in 1914 set the all-time major league mark. Red Sox pitchers with low ERAs include Joe Wood (1.49 in 1915, 1.68 with a losing record in 1910, and 1.91 in 1912). Cy Young had a 1.62 ERA in 1901, 1.97 in 1904, 1.82 in 1905, 1.99 in 1907, and 1.26 in 1908. That makes five seasons of ERAs under 2.00 (his entire career with Boston saw Cy with an ERA of exactly 2.00).

___ **QUESTION 79:** To lead your league in wins, in strikeouts, and earned run average is pitching's Triple Crown. Boston has only had two, and they more or less bracketed the 20th century. Cy Young achieved the feat in 1901 and Pedro Martinez did it in 1999. The very first year of the franchise, after 11 years in the National League, Cy Young was enticed over to join the Boston Americans. He already held a career mark of 286-170. He was coming off a 19-19 year with the St. Louis Cardinals, but posted an outstanding 33-10 mark for Boston, with a 1.62 ERA aided by his 158 strikeouts. Young had 41 starts and threw 38 complete games. He relieved two times. In every game he appeared, he was credited with a win or a loss. He had seven more wins than the second-place finisher, 31 more strikeouts, and the next-closest ERA was almost a full run higher: 2.42. He held batters to an opponents' batting average of .232 and on-base percentage of just .256.

The next Red Sox pitcher to win the Triple Crown was Pedro Martinez, who did so in 1999. Pedro struck out almost twice as many batters as had Cy, whiffing 313 batters. He had an astonishing year, relative to other pitchers in the league. His 23 wins were five more than the second-winningest pitcher, Cleveland's Bartolo Colon. His 313 strikeouts were more than 100 above the #2 man, Chuck Finley, who struck out an even 200 opponents. His ERA of 2.07 was more than a run higher than David Cone of the Yankees, who finished second with 3.44. He posted a strikeouts-to-walks ratio of 8.46; the next closest wasn't even half that, at 3.44 (Felix Heredia). He struck out an average of 13.20 batters per nine innings. Finley came the closest: 8.44. His WHIP (walks plus hits per innings pitched) was .923. Eric Milton's 1.226 was as close as anyone approached Pedro that year. (– from *Red Sox Threads*)

___ **QUESTION 80:** Tim Wakefield, in Detroit on August 8, 2004. He allowed six homers. He's tied for the ML record, one he'd probably just as soon pass up. There was some solace, though – he won the game.

THE MANAGERS, COACHES, ANNOUNCERS, AND TRADES

___ **QUESTION 81:** That the team would win more games than it would lose.

___ **QUESTION 82:** Only one. Chick Stahl committed suicide early in spring training of 1907. The 1906 had been a really, really bad one, but it appears that complications in his love life were likely what drove him to down a drink of carbolic acid, and take his life.

___ **QUESTION 83:** Pinky Higgins was the bad driver. The accident happened on January 15, 1969.

___ **QUESTION 84:** Dave Magadan, who began his tenure as the Red Sox hitting instructor in 2007 – and he finally got a World Series ring, having never won one as a player.

___ **QUESTION 85:** Terry Francona, who has actually led Boston into October five times during his first six seasons with the club, 2004-09.

THE FABULOUS FEATS

___ **QUESTION 86:** Ted Williams, in 1942 and again in 1947 (the only player in the league to ever do it twice), and Carl Yastrzemski in 1967. No one has done it – in either league – since Yaz. Since 1901, it's only been accomplished by eight A.L. players, and three from the National League.

___ **QUESTION 87:** D – the correct answer is 96; see *The Ultimate Red Sox Home Run Guide*.

___ **QUESTION 88:** Just the one that clinched the 1946 pennant, in the 1-0 game on September 13.

___ **QUESTION 89:** Ted Williams – and he accomplished this four times! The biggest margin was in 1941, when he hit 37 homers but only struck out 27 times.

___ **QUESTION 90:** Dwight Evans – 8.

THE TEAMS

___ QUESTION 91: Hard to believe that someone would want that badly to join the Red Sox. Alex Rodriguez was willing to take a $25 million haircut to become a member of the team, but the Players Association refused to allow one of their members to accept such a large trimming and the deal was called off. Since A-Rod's second choice team was willing to pay more, he's now become a much-hated employee of the Evil Empire. But he'd wanted, most of all, at the time, to play for Boston.

___ QUESTION 92: Back on April 20, 1903, Boston's Huntington Avenue Grounds hosted two games on a combined Opening Day/Patriots Day separate admission doubleheader. The 10:00 AM first game is the earliest start of any major league game since the start of the 20th century.

___ QUESTION 93: It was a best-of-nine series, and it took five wins to take the championship. Bill Dinneen threw a four-hit 3-0 shutout to win that final game and Boston won the first World Series ever played.

___ QUESTION 94: Ramiro Mendoza, for the 2004 Red Sox, and more than one from the last century for that New York team.

___ QUESTION 95: The 1918 world championship club, managed by Ed Barrow, won only 75 games during the regular season. The club still posted an impressive .595 winning percentage. Why'd it win so few games? There were only 126 games on the schedule that year. Boston was 75-51 and narrowly beat Cleveland by 2.5 games to win the pennant. Three years later, in 1921, Boston won 75 games again . . . but this time there were 154 games on the schedule, the club lost 79 games, and placed fifth in the pennant race, 23.5 games in back of NY.

MISCELLANEOUS

___ **QUESTION 96:** First baseman Ed Jurak, who did so deliberately, to capture a rat which had been running around and disrupting the game. The mitt showed some bite marks after Jurak – making what some dubbed the "best play of his career" in picking up the rat near the on-deck circle and depositing it in a trash can in the dugout. If you went to a Chinese restaurant that year, you might be reminded that it was the Year of the Rat.

___ **QUESTION 97:** Not exactly, but as part of a deal congruent with the sale of Babe Ruth to New York, the Yankees owners held a mortgage on Fenway Park.

___ **QUESTION 98:** Gladys Heffernan was Joe Cronin's housekeeper.

___ **QUESTION 99:** Selling out every seat in every spring training game at City of Palms Park in Fort Myers since March 16, 2003. Fewer games, but a slightly longer streak.

___ **QUESTION 100:** Red Sox public address announcer Sherm Feller, who also wrote a symphony about John F. Kennedy.

Got your Opening Day total? Here's how it breaks down:

SCOTT BORAS WANTS TO REPRESENT YOU	= 45-50
MLB PLAYER OF THE MONTH FOR APRIL	= 40-44
YOU'RE STILL IN THE SHOW	= 35-39
STRUGGLING TO GET PLAYING TIME	= 30-34
YOU JUST GOT SENT DOWN	= 00-29

Good luck in the All-Star balloting!

Chapter Three

ALL-STAR

SO YOU WANT TO BE AN ALL-STAR, no problem. All you have to do is to bring your "A" game to the park every day, your absolute best, day in, day out, because only a select few make it to that upper echelon where you hear things like "franchise player" or "future Hall of Famer."

(Ted Williams, 1942. Courtesy of the Boston Red Sox)

Oh, and one more thing . . . you have to be better than almost everyone else to make it, which means for some of you, well, your "A" game might not be enough. You better work hard.

I mean, really hard.

You do well here and you will not only have shown us something special, but you will also have earned yourself some well-deserved recognition. Let's get to it.

THE NUMBERS GAME

QUESTION 101: Two Red Sox hitters are among those few who share the record for going 6-for-6 in a major league ballgame. Can you name them?

QUESTION 102: Which man on the Red Sox drove in one or more runs in 12 consecutive games?

QUESTION 103: There are two batters on the Red Sox who have reached base safely 300 or more times in a single season. Who are they?

QUESTION 104: What Red Sox player holds the record for the most runs scored in one inning?

QUESTION 105: Can you name the Red Sox pitcher who balked the most times in a ballgame, tying an American League record?

THE ROOKIES

QUESTION 106: Which Red Sox players won the Rookie of the Year and the MVP in the very same year?

QUESTION 107: Have any other Sox players won both awards?

QUESTION 108: What Sox batter holds the major league record for the most consecutive hits to start off his career?

QUESTION 109: Two Red Sox players accomplished something unusual. Each one of their first three hits were home runs. Who were they?

QUESTION 110: A member of the Red Sox has won Rookie of the Year honors at every infield position except for one – at what infield position has Boston (through 2009) never had a Rookie of the Year recipient?

THE VETERANS

QUESTION 111: Who executed the last unassisted triple play for the Red Sox?

QUESTION 112: True or false: Ted Williams threw out more than 125 baserunners.

QUESTION 113: Who holds the major league record for consecutive hitless innings?

QUESTION 114: What left-hander holds the American League record for the most shutouts in one season?

QUESTION 115: Which of these players never pitched in a Red Sox game?
  a) Tris Speaker
  b) Doc Cramer
  c) Jimmie Foxx
  d) Ted Williams
  e) Steve Lyons

THE LEGENDS

QUESTION 116: What Red Sox outfielder both wrote a book and had a movie made about his life experiences?

QUESTION 117: Almost everyone knows that Ted Williams homered in his last at-bat in the major leagues. Can you name two other players who did the same?

QUESTION 118: Dick Radatz was the Monster – OK, but what was the best relief effort any Red Sox pitcher ever had?

QUESTION 119: Who gave reliever Dick Radatz the nickname "The Monster"?

QUESTION 120: Which Sox player authored a cookbook named *Fowl Tips*?

THE HITTERS

QUESTION 121: Who was the first designated hitter in all of baseball to hit a home run?

QUESTION 122: Which player once hit safely in 12 consecutive at-bats?

QUESTION 123: What Red Sox batter drove in the most runs during one given month?

QUESTION 124: Who hit the most home runs in one inning?

QUESTION 125: Who was the last Red Sox pitcher to hit safely before the DH was instituted?

THE PITCHERS

QUESTION 126: What might be the best season any Red Sox pitcher had, relative to the other pitchers in the league at the time?

QUESTION 127: Name the two pitchers who threw complete games without yielding a hit, but have not been accorded no-hitter status.

QUESTION 128: Which one *lost* his no-hitter? As in, he lost the *game* despite pitching a no-hitter.

QUESTION 129: Can you name the only two pitchers to throw more than one no-hitter for our team?

QUESTION 130: Which one of these pitchers pitched fewer than 40 games for the Boston Red Sox?
   a) Cy Young
   b) Mel Parnell
   c) Ramon Martinez
   d) Joe Dobson

Bonus Question: If you've been paying close attention above, and have committed to memory everything you've learned, you already know the answer to this question: who holds the major league record for the highest number of strikeouts per nine innings pitched, over the course of a season?

The Managers, Coaches, Announcers, and Trades

Question 131: What Red Sox owner said, "The best thing about Boston is the train ride back to New York"?

Question 132: Where was said owner's office located?

Question 133: Who uttered these impassioned words after a crushing Red Sox defeat? "It bothers me that we lost the game."

Question 134: When Boston won 95 games in 2008, manager Terry Francona became the first skipper in franchise history to guide the club to four 90-plus win seasons (and he made it five seasons in 2009). Which manager, who led Boston to three 90-plus win seasons, did Francona surpass in the team record book?

Question 135: A collegiate standout at Oklahoma State and a second-round pick of the Cleveland Indians in 1984, he took over as Red Sox pitching coach in 2007. In his first two seasons in that role the team posted a 3.94 earned run average, which was second best in the league behind the Toronto Blue Jays. Can you name this coach?

THE FABULOUS FEATS

QUESTION 136: Two Red Sox pitchers won both games of a doubleheader. Who were they?

QUESTION 137: Two Red Sox pitchers each threw four consecutive shutouts – please name them.

QUESTION 138: Which Red Sox pitcher won his own no-hitter with a home run?

QUESTION 139: How did the Red Sox do in the first two games against the Yankees after George Steinbrenner took over the New York team?

QUESTION 140: Who was the first player in major-league history to hit a single, a double, and a triple all in the same inning?

THE TEAMS

QUESTION 141: What was the team's longest home winning streak?

QUESTION 142: What year did the Red Sox win the most games in the regular season?

QUESTION 143: Why was it that when the 1914 World Series was held at Fenway Park, the Red Sox did not play?

QUESTION 144: Why was it that when the Red Sox won the pennant in 1915, and again in 1916, neither time did they play a single game at Fenway Park?

QUESTION 145: What Red Sox game featured the most extra-base hits in one game?

MISCELLANEOUS

QUESTION 146: What Sox player's nickname was "Double Cheeseburger"?
 a) Fatty Fothergill
 b) Rich Garces
 c) Reggie Cleveland
 d) Skinny Graham
 e) Kip Gross

QUESTION 147: What was the given name of Red Sox outfielder Colonel Buster Mills?

QUESTION 148: Who were the two top masters of the hidden ball trick for the Red Sox? They each have pulled it off three times.

QUESTION 149: What Red Sox player failed to show up for the last game of winter ball, and was reported kidnapped early in 2005, but turned up 10 days later reporting that he'd merely been away at a beach party?

QUESTION 150: Which Red Sox pitcher led the American League in losses during the same season in which he threw a no-hitter?

Chapter Three Answer Key

Time to find out how you did – put a check mark next to the questions you answered correctly, and when you are done be sure and add up your score to find out your IQ, whether or not you're an All-Star, and to find out if you have a shot at making the postseason.

THE NUMBERS GAME

___ QUESTION 101: On June 10, 1953, Jimmy Piersall went 6-for-6 in the first game of a doubleheader against the St. Louis Browns. The Red Sox won both games, but Piersall was 0-for-5 in the second one. Just a little over 50 years later, on June 21, 2003, Nomar Garciaparra had his 6-for-6 game - every hit a single in a 13-inning game against Philadelphia in Veterans Stadium. Three days later, Nomar had a 5-for-5 game.

___ QUESTION 102: Actually, there were two – Joe Cronin did it in 1939 and Ted Williams did it in 1942.

___ QUESTION 103: Ted Williams did it seven times. Wade Boggs did it six times.

___ QUESTION 104: The major league record is shared by Boston catcher Sammy White, who scored three times in one inning on June 18, 1953.

___ QUESTION 105: John Dopson did this on June 13, 1989 – four times. Once in the first, twice in the second (the last one plating a run), and again in the fourth. The

Red Sox won the game, but the win went to Wes Gardner in relief.

THE ROOKIES

___ **QUESTION 106:** Only one: Fred Lynn, in 1975.

___ **QUESTION 107:** Very recently! Dustin Pedroia won the ROY in 2007 and the MVP in 2008. He is the only other Red Sox player to win both awards.

___ **QUESTION 108:** It's the man who's tied for the Red Sox record for the least number of letters in his first and last names combined – Ted Cox, who hit safely six times in a row on September 18 and 19, 1977. Leading off in the fifth inning of the game on the September 19, though, he grounded out to first base. Over the first seven games of his career, his batting average went down, down, down . . .

___ **QUESTION 109:** It was only in his eighth big league game that Mike Greenwell finally got a hit, but every one of his first three hits were home runs. In the top of the 13th inning of the September 25, 1985, game in Toronto, Bill Buckner doubled and Greenwell followed with a homer off John Cerutti. His hit won the game.

The next day, facing Doyle Alexander and with the Sox down 1-0, Mike Easler singled and – after Dave Stapleton struck out – Greenie homered again, another two-run home run. This one also won the ballgame, a 4-1 final.

After three more games, Greenwell had another hit on October 1 – a ninth-inning solo home run. This time it made no difference at all, boosting the Sox lead over the Orioles to 10-3. All three hits had been on the road. He had three more hits in Baltimore, but his first hit at Fenway was a homer, too, in extra innings on October 4. It wasn't a game-winner, though. The Brewers had scored twice in the top of the 12th.

Ditto Billy Conigliaro – another player whose first hit was a homer. So was his second. They both came in the same game – his third – on April 16, 1969. And, like Greenie, his third hit was a homer, too - the following day. In the process, he struck out five times, but what the heck.

___ **QUESTION 110:** Third base – Don Schwall (P), Carlton Fisk (C), Walt Dropo (1B), Dustin Pedroia (2B), and Nomar Garciaparra (SS) have got the rest of it covered.

THE VETERANS

___ **QUESTION 111:** John Valentin, on July 8, 1994.

___ **QUESTION 112:** True – he threw out 140.

___ **QUESTION 113:** Cy Young, in 1904, threw 25 1/3 hitless innings, one after the other.

___ **QUESTION 114:** George Herman "Babe" Ruth threw nine shutouts in the 1916 season.

___ **QUESTION 115:** Actually, it's a trick question. Sorry about that. They all did.

THE LEGENDS

___ **QUESTION 116:** Jimmy Piersall battled manic depression and wrote about it in his book *Fear Strikes Out*. A movie of the same name was filmed, starring Tony Perkins as Piersall.

___ **QUESTION 117:** Chick Stahl and Don Gile. Stahl did it in the last game of 1906, but then committed suicide during spring training of 1907. Gile hit his final career homer just two years after Ted. *The New Yorker* ran nothing at all on the subject, but Gile suffered not the despondence.

___ **QUESTION 118:** The June 23, 1917, game when Babe Ruth was ejected with a runner on first base and nobody out in the very first inning. Ernie Shore was brought on in relief, picked the runner off first, and then retired the next 26 batters he faced without allowing a single man to reach base. Could there be a more perfect game?

___ **QUESTION 119:** Mickey Mantle. Nick Cafardo says that Mantle often told teammates, "I knew exactly what he was going to throw and where he was going to throw it, and I still couldn't hit it."

___ **QUESTION 120:** Wade Boggs, 1984.

THE HITTERS

___ **QUESTION 121:** Orlando Cepeda on April 8, 1973 – and it won the game against Sparky Lyle in the bottom of the ninth, as the Red Sox won from the Yankees, 4-3.

___ **QUESTION 122:** Pinky Higgins, in 1938. There were two bases on balls mixed in. This stands as tied for the major league record.

___ **QUESTION 123:** Ted Williams drove in 41 runs in the month of May 1942. In June 1950, Ted drove in 40. The surprising flash-in-the-pan Clyde Vollmer drove in 40 during July 1951.

___ **QUESTION 124:** No one's ever hit three, but we hope when someone does, it's a Red Sox batter. Boston's Bill Regan (6/16/28), Ellis Burks (8/27/90), and Nomar Garciaparra (7/23/2002) have each hit two.

___ **QUESTION 125:** On October 3, 1972, Luis Tiant singled off Woodie Fryman of the Tigers in the top of the seventh.

THE PITCHERS

___ **QUESTION 126:** A good argument could be made that it was Pedro Martinez in the 2000 season. He wasn't even a 20-game winner that year (he was 18-6), but then again the Red Sox only won 86 games instead of the 92 they'd won in 1999. Pedro arguably pitched better, though, in 2000. His ERA was just 1.74 (compared to 2.07 the year before and compared to a league average of 4.91), his WHIP was only .737 (compared to .923), his strikeout to walks ratio was 8.88 (better than 1999's 8.46), and he only allowed 5.31 hits per nine innings pitched. Pedro only allowed opposing batters to hit .167 off him, the stingiest performance by a major league pitcher since records began to be kept in the 1800s. His on-base percentage against was .213, the lowest since 1884 (and conditions were so different then as to be questionably comparable). He won himself another unanimous Cy Young Award.

___ **QUESTION 127:** Matt Young and Devern Hansack. Both of them did pitch complete games, and neither of them allowed a hit. What's a no-hitter if that isn't it? Though for different reasons, both games ended before the pitcher in question had to throw nine full innings, and there was an MLB ruling that an "official" no-hitter had to have the pitcher throw a full nine.

___ **QUESTION 128:** On April 12, 1992, Matt Young lost a 2-1 no-hitter to the Indians. That's why he didn't throw the full nine – the game was in Cleveland, and there was no reason for the Indians to bat in the bottom of the ninth since they'd already won the game. Hansack's game was simply rained out after five innings. He won, he threw a game recorded as a shutout, he threw a game recorded as a complete game, and yet . . . he doesn't get "credit" for a no-hitter.

___ **QUESTION 129:** Cy Young – May 5, 1904 (perfect game)   (catcher: Lou Criger); Cy Young – June 30, 1908 (catcher: Lou Criger); Dutch Leonard – August 30, 1916 (catcher: Bill Carrigan); Dutch Leonard – June 3, 1918 (catcher: Wally Schang).

___ **QUESTION 130:** Another trick question. Ramon Martinez only appeared in 31 games for Boston, but you'd have to include Cy Young as well, since he pitched in only 36 games for the Red Sox. The other 291 he pitched for the franchise were all before the team adopted the name "Red Sox."

BONUS QUESTION: Pedro Martinez, who in 1999 averaged 13.2 batters struck out for every nine innings pitched.

THE MANAGERS, COACHES, ANNOUNCERS, AND TRADES

___ **QUESTION 131:** Harry Frazee.

___ **QUESTION 132:** One block away from Col. Ruppert, the principal owner of the New York Yankees, with whom he conducted a very considerable amount of business, most notably the sale of Babe Ruth to the Yankees.

___ **QUESTION 133:** That would be manager Grady Little, after the Red Sox were eliminated in Game Seven of the 2003 American League Championship Series, in 11 innings – on the very brink of going to the World Series for the first time since 1986. Aaron Boone had hit a home run to win the game for the Yankees, in New York. In a moment of further understatement, Little added, "People are going to have opinions about certain decisions that lead to the results of the games. It just bothers me that all they can remember is the last game. That's what bothers me the most." Quite a few Red Sox fans (and the team's new ownership) had some rather strong opinions about one of those decisions. And it was one made in that last game, not Little's decision to remove Pedro Martinez back on June 26 in a game in Detroit when Pedro had allowed a couple of seventh-inning runs to score, cutting the Red Sox lead to 6-3. With the potential tying run coming to the plate, Little called on Alan Embree for help in relief. No, come the morning of October 17, that wasn't the decision that Sox aficionados had fresh in mind. All they could remember was the last game. Though team ownership may have been heartened to know that Little was bothered that the Red Sox had lost Game Seven, they weren't sufficiently swayed to continue his employment.

___ **QUESTION 134:** Bill Carrigan, who came aboard during the 1913 campaign and was 40-30 the rest of the way, and then proceeded to win 91, 101, and 91 games (including two world championships) during his first three full seasons managing the Red Sox – and then he retired. Carrigan came out of retirement to manage Boston for three more seasons from 1927-29, but this time he had little success – *losing* 103, 96, and 96 games.

___ **QUESTION 135:** John Farrell – and his first successes weren't with the Red Sox either. He returned to Oklahoma State as pitching coach from 1997-2001 and developed 14 pitchers at the collegiate level who later pitched professionally – and then he left OSU for Cleveland once again. A one-time prospect with the Indians, he returned to the organization as Director of Player Development, and two years later Baseball America named his farm system the best in professional baseball.

THE FABULOUS FEATS

___ **QUESTION 136:** Ray Collins (1914) and Carl Mays (1919).

___ **QUESTION 137:** Ray Culp (1968) and Luis Tiant (1972). Culp threw 39 scoreless innings in a row and Tiant upped that to 42 1/3.

___ **QUESTION 138:** Earl Wilson, who pitched a no-hitter on June 26, 1962, *and* hit a third-inning homer that day vs. Bo Belinsky of the California Angels.

___ **QUESTION 139:** The Red Sox scored 25 runs and won both games. In fact, the Sox won the third game as well, and then the fourth, after both teams had moved from Boston to Opening Day in New York. Maybe The Boss decided he had better get involved in day-to-day operations. Boston finished the season winning 14 of 18 games from the Yankees. It was 1973.

___ **QUESTION 140:** In the process, Johnny Damon tied the major-league record for hits in an inning, sharing it with Boston's Gene Stephens (June 18, 1953). Damon's feat came on June 27, 2003, and – quite naturally – had everyone hoping he'd come up again and hit a home run. This all happened in the first inning, as the Sox teed off against the visiting Florida Marlins, scoring 14 times in that one inning. Damon had already scored twice before the Red Sox made their first out. The inning might have kept going forever, but on Damon's third hit – the single – Bill Mueller was thrown out at home plate for the third out.

THE TEAMS

___ **QUESTION 141:** It was magic and it happened under manager Joe Morgan, a 24-game winning streak that ran from June 25 through August 13, 1988, embracing two complete home stands and parts of two others. The first one they lost, on August 14, saw Roger Clemens give up eight earned runs in the first 1 1/3 innings.

___ **QUESTION 142:** It was 1912, when they won 105 games – and that was when the teams played 154-games in a season, not the 162 games they have played since 1961. The most they've won since '61 was the 99 wins in 1978, one playoff win shy of the 100 it took that year to win the flag.

___ **QUESTION 143:** They didn't win the pennant. The Boston Braves did, and made arrangements to play in the larger facility.

___ **QUESTION 144:** Even though Fenway was only a few years old, the brand new Braves Field on Commonwealth Avenue was larger. Boston's home games were played at Braves Field both postseasons.

___ **QUESTION 145:** The Sox struck 17 extra-base hits, a major league record, in the game on June 8, 1950.

MISCELLANEOUS

___ **QUESTION 146:** C – it was the Canadian in the group – Reggie Cleveland.

___ **QUESTION 147:** Colonel Buster Mills really did have the given first name of Colonel and the given middle name of Buster.

___ **QUESTION 148:** Johnny Pesky caught Washington's Bill Zuber on May 31, 1942; Johnny Pesky caught New

York's Tommy Henrich on July 4, 1942; and Johnny Pesky caught Washington's Buddy Lewis on July 6, 1947. Marty Barrett caught California's Bobby Grich on July 1, 1985; Marty Barrett (to Glenn Hoffman) caught California's Doug De Cinces on July 21, 1985; and Marty Barrett (to Jody Reed) caught Baltimore's Jim Traber on September 5, 1988.

___ **QUESTION 149:** Venezuela's Rich Garces, the popular relief pitcher known as "El Guapo" – that might have been quite a beach party.

___ **QUESTION 150:** Dave Morehead, who was 9-16 when he threw the no-hitter. After he won that game, he was 10-16 but lost his last two starts. He was tied with Bill Monbouqette with 18 losses, one ahead of Jim Lonborg's 17. The three combined had a W-L record of 29-53. The Mets' Jack Fisher blew them all away with 24 losses that year for the Mets.

Got your All-Star total? Here's how it breaks down:

STARTER WITH MOST FAN VOTES & ALL-STAR GAME MVP	= 45-50
MADE THE TEAM AND WON THE HOME RUN DERBY	= 40-44
YOU MADE IT IN THE FINAL FAN VOTE	= 35-39
YOU'RE THE GUY THAT GOT OVERLOOKED THIS YEAR	= 30-34
YOUR NUMBERS JUST AREN'T GOOD ENOUGH	= 00-29

Good luck down the stretch!

Chapter Four

Dog Days of August

THE SEASON REALLY HEATS UP NOW. The Mid-Summer Classic is behind us, the trade deadline is rapidly approaching, and the race for the postseason is in full throttle.

It's the Dog Days of August.

(Wes Ferrell, 1935. Courtesy of the Boston Red Sox)

This is when cagey veterans make their presence known, the weak begin to fade from contention, and that rare breed of player who just plain knows how to win – or who refuses to lose – achieves baseball immortality with his clutch exploits on the field, at the time of year when every action is magnified, and when his team and its fans need him the absolute most. Think you're that kind of player? We're about to find out . . . it's the Dog Days.

THE NUMBERS GAME

QUESTION 151: Ted Williams hold the record for the highest consecutive number of games in which a baseball player reached base safely. That number is:
   a) 56
   b) 61
   c) 72
   d) 84

QUESTION 152: What was the largest number of men left on base during a shutout?

QUESTION 153: Which man on the Red Sox received the most consecutive bases on balls in one game?

QUESTION 154: The most RBIs by a Red Sox batter in a single game is ten and that's been done four times. Can you name the batters?

QUESTION 155: We know that Smoky Joe Wood's 34 wins in one season is the franchise high. What pitcher holds the record for the most wins in back-to-back seasons?

THE ROOKIES

QUESTION 156: Which Red Sox pitcher threw a no-hitter in his Red Sox debut?
- a)   Mel Parnell
- b)   Billy Rohr
- c)   Clay Buchholz
- d)   Hideo Nomo
- e)   Jon Lester

QUESTION 157: What pitcher walked the bases loaded in his first inning of work in the majors, throwing 15 balls – none of them inside the strike zone – but still threw a shutout?

QUESTION 158: Whose first major league hit was a grand slam?

QUESTION 159: In 1932, this rookie became the first and only Red Sox player with a palindromic last name. At the same time, he also became the first (and so far only) player in franchise history who was born in Poland. Can you name this obscure player?

QUESTION 160: He batted .438 vs. Colorado during the 2007 World Series after playing only 33 games as a rookie during the regular season. Can you name him?

THE VETERANS

QUESTION 161: Who was the last major league ballplayer not to wear a batting helmet?

QUESTION 162: Besides pitching, what other roles did Cy Young perform during Boston baseball games?

QUESTION 163: What Red Sox batting champion never had a regular position (even DH) all year long?

QUESTION 164: This Red Sox player holds the record for the most doubles hit during a big-league career. It's more than 100 doubles more than the second-place man in the American League. Who is it?

QUESTION 165: It's well-known that the Red Sox were the last team in baseball to field an African American ballplayer. What player made a famous speech calling for integration?

THE LEGENDS

QUESTION 166: Which of these Boston ballplayers never hit for the cycle?
  a) Tris Speaker
  b) Ted Williams
  c) Carl Yastrzemski
  d) Jim Rice
  e) Rich Gedman

QUESTION 167: Who is the only player to take part for the Red Sox in four world championship teams?

QUESTION 168: Who is the only Red Sox player to hit for the cycle twice?

QUESTION 169: Who is the most infamous knuckleballer ever to pitch for the Red Sox?

QUESTION 170: What batter hit the most pinch-hit homers in one season?

THE HITTERS

QUESTION 171: Which Red Sox player collected more than 200 hits in each of his first three seasons with the Red Sox?

QUESTION 172: Four of the 11 players to hit two grand slams in the same game have been Red Sox players. One of the other seven, Tony Cloninger, later became the Red Sox pitching coach. Who are the four double-slammers?

QUESTION 173: Who holds the record for the most inside-the-park home runs for the Red Sox?

QUESTION 174: What Red Sox batter hit two pinch-hit homers on the very same day?

QUESTION 175: In terms of runs batted in during a single season, who was the most productive pinch-hitter in baseball history?

THE PITCHERS

QUESTION 176: For a pitcher, strikeouts are good and bases on balls are bad. Which pitcher had the best strikeouts-to-walk ratio, and which had the worst?

QUESTION 177: It certainly doesn't happen much today, since only interleague play in National League parks really offers the opportunity, but can you name the two pitchers who have hit walk-off HRs for the Red Sox?

QUESTION 178: Was there ever a Red Sox pitcher who retired all three batters in an inning with just three pitches?

QUESTION 179: How about opening a ballgame by throwing nine straight strikes and recording three outs?

QUESTION 180: Which Red Sox pitcher on the 1967 team won his last eight decisions?
    a) Jim Lonborg
    b) Jose Santiago
    c) Gary Bell
    d) John Wyatt

THE MANAGERS, COACHES, ANNOUNCERS, AND TRADES

QUESTION 181: They used to be fairly common, but it's been a while since we've seen one anywhere in baseball – and it would probably be impossible in the era of free agency. After all, can one man be labor and management at the same time? Who was the last player-manager on the Red Sox?

QUESTION 182: Which Red Sox manager won the highest percentage of games he skippered?
    a) Jake Stahl
    b) Joe Cronin
    c) Dom Zimmer
    d) Terry Francona
    e) Steve O'Neill

QUESTION 183: Who's the only manager in Red Sox history to take the team to the World Series two years in a row?

QUESTION 184: Which two men managed the team the year they recorded more than 100 wins and the year they suffered more than 100 losses?

QUESTION 185: Only three Boston A.L. skippers have been at the helm for as many as five consecutive full seasons. Terry Francona is obviously one of them – but who are the other two?

THE FABULOUS FEATS

QUESTION 186: Roger Clemens struck out 20 batters in a game not just once, but twice. The first time was in 1986 and the second was more than ten years later, in September 1996. What were three significant things about the second 20-K game that distinguish it from the first?

QUESTION 187: Six runs batted in during one inning remains the major league record. Two Red Sox have accomplished this feat, and neither of them are among the four who drove in ten runs in a game. Can you name the two who drove in six?

QUESTION 188: There have been five times a pitcher has won more than 25 games in a single season for Boston.

Can you identify the pitchers from the following list of ten?

    a) Roger Clemens
    b) Smoky Joe Wood
    c) Cy Young
    d) Pedro Martinez
    e) Tex Hughson
    f) Mel Parnell
    g) John Wasdin
    h) Babe Ruth
    i) Wes Ferrell
    j) Boo Ferriss

QUESTION 189: When Boggs hit 207 times in 1986, he also walked 105 times. Who was the last major league player to reach the 200/100 mark in a single season?

QUESTION 190: Who holds the record (also a tie) for the most pinch hits in one inning?

THE TEAMS

QUESTION 191: What was the very worst season in franchise history, in terms of wins and losses?

QUESTION 192: The 1904 team won the American League pennant but never played a single game in the World Series. Why was that?

QUESTION 193: True or false: Boston once played an official game on meadows once used for public hangings and known as Jailhouse Flats, in Fort Wayne, Indiana.

QUESTION 194: What was the very unusual way the Red Sox started the 1969 season?

QUESTION 195: What is the largest crowd before which the Red Sox have ever played?

MISCELLANEOUS

QUESTION 196: What Red Sox player holds the major league record for assists by a first baseman?

QUESTION 197: Which Red Sox player took part in the most double plays of any?

QUESTION 198: Can you name three Red Sox players who played pro football?

QUESTION 199: Was there a pitcher who lost a game without the opposition ever recording an at-bat?

QUESTION 200: What Sox pitcher was stabbed to death at the going-away party intended to see him off to spring training?

Chapter Four Answer Key

Time to find out how you did – put a check mark next to the questions you answered correctly, and when you are done be sure and add up your score to find out your IQ, and . . . most importantly, how you did down the stretch.

THE NUMBERS GAME

___ **QUESTION 151:** D – the answer is 84. It staggers the imagination, but starting on July 1, 1949, Williams got on base at least once in every game through September 27. He played each and every game of the entire season.

___ **QUESTION 152:** The Sox were shut out by Oakland, 3-0, on May 16, 1988. With seven hits and seven walks, they got runners on base, but left *14* men on.

___ **QUESTION 153:** It's sometimes hard to measure intent, since a pitcher may just be pitching very carefully while not providing anything near the strike zone, but Jimmie Foxx was walked six times in a row in the June 16, 1938, game against the Browns. He shows up in the box score as 0-for-0 with two runs scored.

___ **QUESTION 154:** Rudy York – July 27, 1946; Norm Zauchin – May 27, 1955 (10.75% of his year's production all in just one day); Fred Lynn – June 18, 1975; and Nomar Garciaparra – May 10, 1999.

___ **QUESTION 155:** Babe Ruth won 23 games in 1916 and 24 in 1917. Not one Red Sox pitcher has matched the total of 47 in back-to-back seasons since Ruth. Clemens came closer than anyone else with 24 in 1986 and 20 in 1987. Of course, not even Ruth could top Cy Young, who won 33 in 1901 and 32 in 1902, for a total of 65! And then he won 28 in 1903 and . . . obviously continuing to decline from one year to the next, only 26 in 1904.

THE ROOKIES

___ **QUESTION 156:** D – it was Hideo Nomo, his second no-hitter in the big leagues but his first in the A.L. Buchholz's no-no came in his second start. Parnell's only came in his final year with the Red Sox.

___ **QUESTION 157:** Boo Ferriss, 1945.

___ **QUESTION 158:** As with Greenwell, Creighton Gubanich had to wait a bit for his first hit but when it came, it was a big one. Gubanich appeared in two early-season games in 1989, first as a defensive replacement without an at-bat and second as a starting catcher (0-for-3). On May 3, he got his second start and hit a grand slam home run in the top of the first inning in Oakland. It was the only home run he ever hit in his brief 18-game major league career.

___ **QUESTION 159:** Johnny Reder, who played just 17 major league games.

___ **QUESTION 160:** Jacoby Ellsbury, who was 7-for-16 with four doubles, four runs, and three RBIs as Boston defeated Colorado to win the World Series.

THE VETERANS

___ **QUESTION 161:** Bob Montgomery, who was among those grandfathered in when the rule changed and helmets were required.

___ **QUESTION 162:** He served as a coach, a ticket taker, an umpire (by mutual consent of the other team), and even was a pinch-runner – twice in the same game!

___ **QUESTION 163:** Billy Goodman, 1950. He played 27 games at third base, 21 at first, five games at second base, and one at shortstop. He played 45 games in the outfield.

___ **QUESTION 164:** Tris Speaker, with 792.

___ **QUESTION 165:** Ted Williams devoted part of his acceptance speech during 1966 induction ceremonies at the National Baseball Hall of Fame to call for the inclusion of former Negro League greats such as Satchel Paige and Josh Gibson.

THE LEGENDS

___ **QUESTION 166:** D – Jim Rice never hit for a cycle.

___ **QUESTION 167:** Harry Hooper. We do hope someone will soon beat that record!

___ **QUESTION 168:** Bobby Doerr – May 17, 1944, and May 13, 1947.

___ **QUESTION 169:** Eddie Cicotte, who later won more than 20 games three times for the White Sox before being banned for life in the Black Sox scandal. Cicotte won 51 games for the Red Sox.

___ **QUESTION 170:** Joe Cronin, who hit five pinch-hit homers in 1943. It remains the American League record.

THE HITTERS

___ **QUESTION 171:** Johnny Pesky, in 1942, 1946, and 1947 – the latter two seasons coming only after being out of baseball for three years while serving in the Navy during World War II.

___ **QUESTION 172:** Jim Tabor – July 4, 1939; Rudy York – July 27, 1946; Nomar Garciaparra – May 10, 1999; and Bill Mueller – July 29, 2003.

___ **QUESTION 173:** Hobe Ferris hit 24, but the answer is Tris Speaker, who had 25 IPHRs.

___ **QUESTION 174:** Joe Cronin, on June 17, 1943. Both were three-run blasts, one in each game of the doubleheader against St. Louis. Just two days earlier, he'd hit another pinch-hit three-run homer.

___ **QUESTION 175:** Joe Cronin is tied for the major league record for the most pinch-hit RBIs in one season: 25, in 1943.

THE PITCHERS

___ **QUESTION 176:** Through 2007, Curt Schilling had the best ratio of strikeouts to walks (4.38 to 1) of any major league pitcher since 1900 who had thrown at least 2,000 innings. Second on the list is Pedro Martinez with a 4:28-1 ratio. In both cases, much of their pitching was done for other teams. Fortunately, both were on the 2004 Red Sox.

The worst season ratio for a Red Sox pitcher was Ted Wingfield's 1 to 27, in 1927. Wingfield pitched 74 2/3 innings and struck out – yes – just one man all year long. He faced 346 batters, walked 27, and allowed 105 hits. No wild pitches all year. No balks. Just one strikeout, on August 10 – Athletics shortstop Chick Galloway.

___ **QUESTION 177:** As best we can reconstruct, it has only happened four times in the first 107 years of Red Sox history, and all four times were packed into the space of 377 days:
  - Wes Ferrell – August 22, 1934
  - Wes Ferrell – July 21, 1935
  - Wes Ferrell – July 22, 1935
  - Jack Wilson – September 2, 1935

And guess who the starting pitcher was the day Jack Wilson hit his? Wes Ferrell.

___ **QUESTION 178:** It's only happened about three dozen times in major league history. Sonny Siebert did it for the Red Sox on May 11, 1969, throwing three pitches in the second inning of the game against California.

___ **QUESTION 179:** Pedro Martinez opened the May 18, 2002, ballgame against the Seattle Mariners with nine straight strikes for three strikeouts. This is not an easy thing to do. There can be foul balls, of course, but never a foul on the third pitch of the at-bat, unless it's a tip right into the catcher's mitt. He's the only pitcher in American League history (through 2009) ever to have opened a game with three straight strikeouts on nine pitches.

___ **QUESTION 180:** B – Santiago was 4-4 on July 5, and then he reeled off eight wins in eight decisions to finish 12-4 in a season when the pennant was won on the very last day.

THE MANAGERS, COACHES, ANNOUNCERS, AND TRADES

___ **QUESTION 181:** Lou Boudreau, 1952-54.

___ **QUESTION 182:** A – Jake Stahl, who won a heckuva lot of them. Percentages? Stahl managed just one and a half seasons (1912-13), winning 62.1% of the games. Steve O'Neill won 60.6% and Joe McCArthy won 60.2%. No other manager has yet reached the 60% mark, other than Eddie Popowski, who won six of the whopping ten games he managed.

___ **QUESTION 183:** Bill Carrigan (1915-16).

___ **QUESTION 184:** Jake Stahl (1912) 105-47, and Lee Fohl (1926) 46-107.

___ **QUESTION 185:** Joe Cronin (13, 1935-47) and Jimmy Collins (5, 1901-05).

THE FABULOUS FEATS

___ **QUESTION 186:** For one thing, it was the last game he ever won for the Red Sox. He started twice more, but won neither game. Secondly, the win gave Clemens 192 wins with the Red Sox, tying him with Cy Young for the most wins of any Red Sox pitcher. Lastly, the 4-0 game was his 38th shutout for the Red Sox, which also tied him with Mr. Young for the most shutouts for the team.

___ **QUESTION 187:** Carlos Quintana on July 30, 1991 - helping the Red Sox break out of their worst home slump in over 60 years. Tom McBride did it for the Red Sox, too, back on August 4, 1945.

___ **QUESTION 188:** B & C – it's a bit of a trick question. Joe Wood won 34 games in 1912. All four other seasons, the pitcher was Cy Young. No other pitcher has won more than 25 games in a given year. Young's win totals declined over his first four years – 33 (1901), 32 (1902), 28 (1903), and 26 (1904).

___ **QUESTION 189:** Stan Musial, in 1953.

___ **QUESTION 190:** Russ Nixon does. On May 4, 1962, the Red Sox were losing 4-0 to Chicago, had a runner on first and one out in the bottom of the first inning. Nixon was sent up to bat for pitcher Mike Fornieles. He singled. Three batters later, he scored. Four walks and five singles later, he came up again and singled again.

And scored again, too. By the time the inning was over, the Red Sox held a 12-4 lead. They won the game.

THE TEAMS

___   **QUESTION 191:** There was certainly no heartbreaking defeat on the final day of the season, but in 1906, the Boston Americans won just 49 games and lost 105. This included a 19-game home losing streak. The longest winning streak of the season was a euphoric four-game stretch in August.

___ **QUESTION 192:** The 1904 New York Giants shared the sentiment of many teams in the "senior circuit" that the upstart American League was inferior, and that they should not lower themselves to playing the winner of the A.L. in the postseason. So they refused to take part in any World Series that year.

___ **QUESTION 193:** That's such an absurd question that the answer must be true, right?   Right. On Sunday, August 31, 1902, some 3,500 Fort Wayne fans turned out for what proved to be an exciting 11-inning game between the Boston and Cleveland clubs, Cy Young beating Addie Joss, 3-1.

___ **QUESTION 194:** On April 8, 10, & 11, 1969 the Red Sox started the '69 season with three extra-inning games, each one running longer than the one before – 12 innings, 13 innings, and 16 innings. The first two were in Baltimore, the third in Cleveland. The Red Sox lost the middle game, the 13-inning affair.

___ **QUESTION 195:** March 30, 2008: The Red Sox played before the largest crowd ever to watch a baseball game, some 115,300 who thronged the Los Angeles Coliseum to witness an exhibition game between the 2007 World Champion Boston Red Sox and the Los Angeles Dodgers celebrating the 50th anniversary of their move from Brooklyn to L.A.

MISCELLANEOUS

___ **QUESTION 196:** Bill Buckner, 184 in 1985.

___ **QUESTION 197:** Oddly, it wasn't a first baseman. The answer is Bobby Doerr, who is credited with taking part in 1,507 DPs.

___ **QUESTION 198:** There are more than three right answers – you could have said any of the following: Dick Reichle, Jack Perrin, Hoge Workman, Charlie Berry, Bill McWilliams, Carroll Hardy.

___ **QUESTION 199:** There have likely been a few. We know of at least this one. Starting the second game of the April 21, 1946, doubleheader, Jim Bagby Jr. walked the first four Athletics he faced. He was pulled from the mound, but had already forced in the run granting Philadelphia all the edge they needed in a 3-0 ballgame. The A's had not officially registered even one at-bat against Bagby.

___ **QUESTION 200:** Pitcher Big Ed Morris, in 1932.

Got your Dog Days total? Here's how it breaks down:

WON THE PENNANT AND NLCS MVP HONORS	= 45-50
WON THE PENNANT IN A THRILLING SEVEN-GAME SERIES	= 40-44
DIVISION CHAMPION	= 35-39
LATE SEASON SLUMP BUT YOU GOT THE WILD CARD	= 30-34
SITTING HOME THIS OCTOBER	= 00-29

Good luck in October!

Chapter Five

OCTOBER BASEBALL

IT ALL COMES DOWN TO THIS. You spent your childhood dreaming of this moment.

(Carlton Fisk, 1975. Courtesy of the Boston Red Sox)

It's October baseball.

This is your one chance at baseball immortality. You're the underdog. No one expected you to make it this far, but at least to this point you've proved them all wrong. The only thing left to prove is that you have what it takes to be a world champion. No need to be nervous – it's not like we saved the 50 toughest questions for last or anything.

THE NUMBERS GAME

QUESTION 201: The Red Sox hold the record for the most batters reaching first base in one inning. How many batters was that, and when did this great day occur?

QUESTION 202: What catcher once threw out six would-be basestealers in one game?

QUESTION 203: Which Sox player could be said to be the most lightweight one ever?

QUESTION 204: What is the major league record for assists in one inning?

QUESTION 205: What uniform number did future Hall of Famer Rollie Fingers wear when he was a member of the Red Sox?

THE ROOKIES

QUESTION 206: Who was the former Negro League player who played for the Red Sox in 1925 and 1926, more than 20 years before Jackie Robinson's debut, and then returned to the Negro Leagues after his stint with the Red Sox?

QUESTION 207: What was one of the most dramatic debuts of any Red Sox player?

QUESTION 208: There was a Red Sox player who drove in a run without even one at-bat, then waited five years until his next RBI – and he wasn't a pitcher. Who was he?

QUESTION 209: There are three Red Sox pitchers who surrendered a home run to the very first batter they ever faced in major league ball. Who were they?

QUESTION 210: What player (no, it's not a pitcher) failed to get a hit for the Red Sox until into his *fourth* season with the team?

THE VETERANS

QUESTION 211: Lou Gehrig's streak of playing in 2,130 consecutive games was broken by Cal Ripken in 1995. Whose streak did Gehrig break?

QUESTION 212: What shortstop averaged 51 errors over a seven-year stretch with the Red Sox, but kept getting the job back year after year?

QUESTION 213: What Boston player went on to become president of a university?

QUESTION 214: What Hall of Famer holds the record for the most losses in a single season by a Red Sox pitcher?

QUESTION 215: Who holds the highest legitimate* single-season on-base percentage of the 20th century?

THE LEGENDS

QUESTION 216: Former President Bush stumped Senator Edward Kennedy with this one, asking who was the only pitcher to ever strike out Ted Williams three times in a single game. What was the correct answer?

QUESTION 217: What Red Sox player began his professional baseball career playing ball while dressed as a woman?

QUESTION 218: Which pitcher recorded the most consecutive wins to start the season? This pitcher ran his record to 14-0 before losing his first game.

QUESTION 219: Which Red Sox ballplayer was notably granted an audience before Pope Pius X?

QUESTION 220: What year did the Red Sox have two 200-hit batters?

THE HITTERS

QUESTION 221: Was there someone who appeared in eight games for the 2007 Red Sox but could arguably be said to have made a negative contribution to the team's playoff run?

QUESTION 222: What Boston ballplayer holds the record for the most triples hit in one game?

QUESTION 223: Which Red Sox batter had the most 200-hit seasons?
  a) Ted Williams
  b) Carl Yastrzemski
  c) Jim Rice
  d) Wade Boggs
  e) Nomar Garciaparra

QUESTION 224: Is it safe to say that Fenway Park is a home-run haven?

QUESTION 225: OK, so what's the fewest number of homers hit *at home* by the Red Sox in any given year?

THE PITCHERS

QUESTION 226: Who was the last Red Sox pitcher to throw a legal spitball?

QUESTION 227: What pitcher holds the unfortunate record of the most losses in a row for Boston?

QUESTION 228: What pitcher threw a complete game shutout in his last major league appearance?

QUESTION 229: During a game on May 20, 1948, Red Sox pitchers allowed a record large number of bases on balls. How many walks did they dole out?

QUESTION 230: What horror novelist wrote a book that included the name of a Red Sox pitcher?

THE MANAGERS, COACHES, ANNOUNCERS, AND TRADES

QUESTION 231: Who was the first Native American manager on the Red Sox?

QUESTION 232: When was Joe Torre very close to becoming manager of the Boston Red Sox?

QUESTION 233: Bill Werle threw nine balls in a row, so the Boston manager replaced the catcher! Who was the catcher?

QUESTION 234: Prior to Terry Francona in 2007, who was the last Red Sox manager to lead Boston to an A.L. East title?

QUESTION 235: This third base coach spent four years as an instructor at the Bucky Dent Baseball School in Boca Raton, FL, before seeing the light and taking on managerial duties for the Red Sox at Single-A Ft. Lauderdale in 1993. A former Red Sox prospect, he began his tenure as the Red Sox third base coach in 2006. Can you name him?

THE FABULOUS FEATS

QUESTION 236: Can you name the two franchise pitchers who have won three games during a single World Series for the Red Sox?

QUESTION 237: There was one year when one pitcher won three of the season's first four games. Who was it?
  a) Bill Dinneen
  b) Bill Landis
  c) Bill Monbouquette
  d) Boo Ferriss
  e) Dick Radatz

QUESTION 238: It should come as no surprise that Cy Young threw more complete games than any other Red

Sox pitcher. Who are #2 and #3 on that list?
- a) Pedro Martinez
- b) George Winter
- c) Bill Dinneen
- d) Roger Clemens
- e) Luis Tiant

QUESTION 239: Did the Red Sox ever have a player who went through an entire season, with more than 1,000 chances and never once committed an error at his position?

QUESTION 240: This Red Sox player hit only one home run during 49 games to start 2009, but when the club was in need of a spark to get its postseason push into gear, he stepped it up and blasted 25 homers in 92 games from June 6 through September 25, giving him the highest total in the league during that span. Can you name this Red Sox star?

THE TEAMS

QUESTION 241: The 1960 Red Sox traded for the same player twice during the same year. Can you name this player?

QUESTION 242: The 1916 club played the longest scoreless game in franchise history. How many innings did that game last?

QUESTION 243: What was the biggest skunking the Sox ever suffered in a single day, and . . . which team was it that made the Sox look so bad?

QUESTION 244: The 1946 club came oh so close to winning the World Series. Who "held the ball" during a crucial play in the 1946 World Series?

QUESTION 245: The 1978 club came oh so close to winning the division. And you know what happened during the one-game playoff vs. the Yankees . . . but do you know what Bucky Dent's real middle name is? No, it isn't . . .

MISCELLANEOUS

QUESTION 246: What strange move did the Red Sox make just three months after they won their fourth World Series?

QUESTION 247: What former Red Sox player has been executive director of the Jimmy Fund for 30 years?

QUESTION 248: Four players have caught multiple no-hitters for the Red Sox. How many of those catchers can you name?

QUESTION 249: The Boston Americans set a league record that's stood since 1901 for getting the most consecutive hits. Exactly how many consecutive hits did Boston get to set this long-standing record?

QUESTION 250: There has only been one time that a woman pitched against the Red Sox. Who was it?

Chapter Five Answer Key

Time to find out how you did – put a check mark next to the questions you answered correctly, and when you are done be sure and add up your score to find out your IQ, and whether or not you've earned a world championship ring!

THE NUMBERS GAME

___ **QUESTION 201:** It's a major league record. A full 20 batters reached base in one inning, on June 18, 1953.

___ **QUESTION 202:** Wally Schang, in a game in 1916.

___ **QUESTION 203:** In *The Sporting News* of October 29, 1942, Everett Scott said, "I weighed 125 pounds when I started as a regular with the Red Sox in 1914, and I never tipped the scales at more than 138 pounds in the 13 years I played in the majors."

___ **QUESTION 204:** Ten, set by the Red Sox (thanks to two rundowns) in the fifth inning of the May 10, 1952, game against the Yankees (there could have been two more, but scoring rules prevent a fielder from receiving credit for more than one assist on a given play).

___ **QUESTION 205:** None. Officially, he never was a member of the Red Sox. After he was sold to the Red Sox on June 15, 1976, he was assigned – and wore - #34, but the sale was voided three days later, before he ever appeared in a game. Officially, he never was a member of the Red Sox.

THE ROOKIES

___ QUESTION 206: Havana native Ramon "Mike" Herrera.

___ QUESTION 207: It was sure a good way to make an impression on your new team. On June 15, 1947, Jake Jones, in his first game with his new team (the Red Sox) beat up on his old team (the White Sox). His first appearance for Boston came in a doubleheader. Jones homered in the first game, a solo shot that helped Boston beat Chicago, 7-3. In the second game, he came up with two outs and the bases loaded in the bottom of the ninth, the game a 4-4 tie. Grand slam.

___ QUESTION 208: On August 13, 1955, Jim Pagliaroni made his major league debut, at age 17 the youngest player to ever appear for the Red Sox. When the Senators built up a 17-6 lead over the Sox, he was put in to spell Sammy White behind the plate and caught a couple of innings. He never did get an at-bat, but he picked up an RBI with a sacrifice fly. It was more than five years later before he appeared in another major league game, but ended up playing 11 years in major league ball.

___ QUESTION 209: Charlie Mitchell came in to pitch the eighth inning of the August 9, 1984, night game at Arlington Stadium. First Ranger up was first baseman Pete O'Brien, who homered. Mitchell then retired the next three batters. It was one of only two home runs Mitchell ever surrendered – but then again he only ever pitched 18 innings in the major leagues.

Jeff Suppan built a long career in major league ball, but it started with a leadoff homer by Kansas City second baseman Keith Lockhart on July 17, 1995, at Fenway Park. Suppan got out of the inning, and pitched 5 2/3 innings but bore the loss as the Royals won the game, 4-3.

Hideki Okajima's came in relief on Opening Day 2007. Taking the ball to throw the bottom of the sixth, he threw his first pitch to Kansas City catcher John Buck – who drove it out of the park.

___ **QUESTION 210:** Haywood Sullivan played for the Red Sox in 1955, 1957, and 1959 without collecting even one base hit. His first hit came in his second game of 1960, an April 19 single.

THE VETERANS

___ **QUESTION 211:** Everett Scott, who broke in with the Red Sox in 1914 and appeared in 1,307 consecutive games (June 20, 1916 - May 6, 1925), spanning seasons with both the Red Sox and the Yankees.

___ **QUESTION 212:** Heinie Wagner, 1907-13. Not only that, he played in parts of four other seasons and was later made manager.

___ **QUESTION 213:** Ted Lewis was president of the University of New Hampshire.

___ **QUESTION 214:** Red Ruffing, who was 10-25 in 1928.

___ **QUESTION 215:** Ted Williams, with a .553 on-base percentage in 1941*. There's an asterisk next to this one, however, because in 2002, Barry Bonds had an on-base percentage of .582, in the year after he hit 73 home runs. Indicted by a Federal grand jury in November 2007, it remains to be seen whether allegations of cheating through the use of illegal steroids tainted several of the records set by Bonds. We're not hesitant to use an asterisk to draw attention to the question.

THE LEGENDS

___ **QUESTION 216:** U.S. Senator Jim Bunning (R-KY) did so on May 16, 1957. His fourth time up, in the ninth inning, Ted doubled and scored, but it was still a 2-1 loss to the Tigers.

___ **QUESTION 217:** No, this wasn't some rookie hazing ritual. Smoky Joe Wood began his professional baseball career playing for a Bloomer Girls ballclub. Wood was assigned the name "Lucy Tolton," fitted for a wig, and decked out in bloomers. Odd as it may seem, there were a number of other ballplayers (Rogers Hornsby comes to mind) who also played on the Bloomer Girls teams in the early part of the 20th century.

___ **QUESTION 218:** Roger Clemens, kicking off the 1986 season. He didn't lose a game in April, May, or June. After the first half of the season, Clemens' record was 14-0. It was only on July 2, and only in the top of the eighth in a 4-2 game against Toronto, that Rocket Roger lost his first game. Clemens finished the season 24-4.

___ QUESTION **219:** On February 11, 1914, Tris Speaker was among touring major league ballplayers granted an audience at the Vatican before Pope Pius X. This was ironic in that Speaker was one of the Masons on a Red Sox team somewhat divided between Catholics and anti-Catholics.

___ QUESTION **220:** In 1986, they had both Jim Rice and Wade Boggs.

THE HITTERS

___ QUESTION **221:** That would be a little unkind, but is statistically correct on offense. In 2007, Royce Clayton won himself a World Championship ring. The well-traveled infielder was playing for his record 11th major league team. At the plate, his contribution to the Red Sox was a negative 100 OPS+. He had six at-bats, without a hit, struck out three times, and grounded into two double plays. But he did score a run. And was perfect in the field with two assists in the only two chances he got.

___ QUESTION **222:** In earlier days, when overflow crowds were permitted to stand in the outfield behind ropes, balls hit into the crowd were typically scored as either doubles or triples, per the ground rules announced before the day's game. The ground rule helped Patsy Dougherty hit three triples in one game (he hit two singles, too) on September 5, 1903 – and this was in a game called due to rain after 7 1/2 innings.

___ **QUESTION 223:** D – Wade Boggs. Neither Ted nor Yaz ever reached 200. Ted's highest total was 194 (1949) and Yaz's was 191 (1962). Nomar hit safely 209 times in 1997. Jim Rice hit 200 or more hits four times – 1977, 1978, 1979, and 1986. Boggs did it seven years in a row, from 1983 through 1987.

___ **QUESTION 224:** Not at all. Despite the inviting left-field wall, that wall is tall! Many a ball that would have been a homer elsewhere is a double – or even a single. David Vincent did a study for *The Ultimate Red Sox Home Run Guide*, which demonstrated that since 1985, the number of homers hit at Fenway has generally been below that of the other American League ballparks.

___ **QUESTION 225:** Incredible but true! The 1916 world champion Red Sox hit only one home run all year long in their home ballpark.

Tillie Walker, playing for the St. Louis Browns had hit one on September 24, 1915 – and that was the last home run hit at Fenway until June 20, 1916. Oddly enough, it was Tillie Walker who hit the June 20 one – although now he was playing for the Red Sox. Walker hit three in all during 1916, but this was the only one he – or any Red Sox player – hit at Fenway.

In 1918, when he led the American League with 11 home runs, Babe Ruth hit every one of them on the road.

THE PITCHERS

___ QUESTION 226: Jack Quinn. When the pitch was outlawed in 1920, he was one of several spitballers who were grandfathered in to allow them to use it throughout their careers. Quinn last used it for Boston in 1925, but kept pitching until 1933, six days after he turned 50.

___ QUESTION 227: Joe Harris was winless during his first 15 starts in 1906. He'd won his last game in 1905. After his August 8, 1906, win he lost his next 13 decisions and the team finally decided it had seen enough. Harris finished his major league career with a lifetime record of 3-30. That's not a typo. That is three wins and 30 losses.

___ QUESTION 228: Even rarer than hitting a home run in your final at-bat in the major leagues is throwing a shutout in your last game. Brian Denman is one of just five pitchers to do this. Denman shut out the Yankees, 5-0, on October 2, 1982. It was a six-hitter at Yankee Stadium. Denman improved his record to 3-4 and closed his only major league season with a 4.78 earned run average. He pitched 49 innings in all, and was 0-for-9 at the plate. He never returned to the big leagues.

___ QUESTION 229: Eighteen. That's right, the equivalent of giving everyone in the lineup two walks apiece. And it only took two pitchers to do it! Mickey Harris gave seven, and Mickey McDermott handed out 11. This unparalleled generosity – not surprisingly - cost the Red Sox the game. Though Bob Lemon walked five Boston batters, the Sox lost to the Indians, 13-4.

___ **QUESTION 230:** "I think it's an unbelievable thing. I've always enjoyed Stephen King's work. My whole family is a fan of his," said Red Sox closer Tom Gordon in 1999 on being asked about King's new novel published by Scribner's, *The Girl Who Loved Tom Gordon.* King is a lifelong Sox fan, since his first game in 1959.

THE MANAGERS, COACHES, ANNOUNCERS, AND TRADES

___ **QUESTION 231:** Rudy York. The Boston Red Sox, last team in the majors to have an African-American player on their team, may have been the first to have a Native American manager. If only for one day. "I'm a Cherokee Indian, and I'm proud of it," York proclaimed. He was 1/8 Cherokee, but identified as "Indian" and was understood by his fellow players to be a Native American. He managed the Boston Red Sox in 1959. For one day. July 3, 1959. The Sox had fired Pinky Higgins, asked York to manage the game while they sought a replacement. Three hours later, they hired Billy Jurges, but York still skippered the game that day, and lost to the Orioles 6-1, when Baltimore piled up five first-inning runs off starter Jack Harshman.

___ **QUESTION 232:** In the first half of the 1988 season, Torre was working as a broadcaster with KTLA in Los Angeles. The Red Sox were dissatisfied with John McNamara as manager and Boston GM Lou Gorman gave Torre a call to sound him out. In April 2004, Torre recalled, "[Gorman] said they weren't sure what they were going to do but by the All-Star break they'd make a decision. They didn't fire Mac till after the All-Star break, they hired Joe Morgan in the interim, and he won about 12 or 13 in a row. Lou Gorman called me and said, `Well, that's that.' I sent him a box of cigars and said thanks for thinking about me." [*Boston Globe*, April 15, 2004]

___ QUESTION 233: Sammy White, 1954.

___ QUESTION 234: Kevin Kennedy, 1995.

___ QUESTION 235: DeMarlo Hale.

THE FABULOUS FEATS

___ QUESTION 236: Bill Dinneen in 1903 and Smoky Joe Wood in 1912.

___ QUESTION 237: B – Bill Landis, in 1969, won the first, third, and fourth game of the season. The next game he won was on June 27. His record on the year: 5-5.

___ QUESTION 238: Young threw 275 CG. Dinneen (156) and Winter (141) were second and third. Joe Wood (121) and Lefty Grove (119) round out the top five. Tiant tied with Mel Parnell at 113, Clemens threw an even 100, and Pedro pitched 22. Even Babe Ruth topped Roger, with 105 complete games.

___ QUESTION 239: Kevin Youkilis played the full 2007 season without making an error at first base, even though given 1,080 chances in which to do so.

___ QUESTION 240: David Ortiz, of course.

THE TEAMS

___ **QUESTION 241:** Russ Nixon, on March 16 and on June 13, 1960. The first trade was voided when Sammy White refused to report to the Indians.

___ **QUESTION 242:** The July 14, 1916, game was called on account of darkness after 17 scoreless innings.

___ **QUESTION 243:** It was the Cleveland Indians on June 23, 1931. It was a doubleheader, in Cleveland. The Indians took the first game 13-0 and won the nightcap 10-0, for a total score on the day of 23-0.

___ **QUESTION 244:** No one, really. Instead of looking for someone to blame, all credit for pulling off the play goes to Enos Slaughter. Legend has it that Sox shortstop Johnny Pesky held a relay throw too long, enabling Slaughter to score from second base on a double by Harry Walker. Two existing films of the play make clear what all the players present, and legendary St. Louis sportswriter Bob Broeg all agreed: it was too late to get Slaughter at the plate. He was almost at second base before contact and his "mad dash" around third to home caught just-installed center fielder Leon Culberson lobbing the ball in after what appeared to be a purely routine play.

___ **QUESTION 245:** Earl.

MISCELLANEOUS

___ **QUESTION 246:** On January 19, 1916, following their World Championship in 1915, the Red Sox took advantage of the occasion to . . . *lower* their ticket prices.

___ **QUESTION 247:** Former second baseman Mike Andrews, who joined the Jimmy Fund in 1973 and has been executive director since 1979.

___ **QUESTION 248:** Lou Criger, Bill Carrigan, Bob Tillman, and Jason Varitek.

___ **QUESTION 249:** Ten – on June 2, 1901.

___ **QUESTION 250:** On March 22, 1934, the starting pitcher facing the Red Sox was "girl Olympic star" Babe Didrikson, who threw the first inning of the day's exhibition game in Bradenton, Florida, for the St. Louis Cardinals. This particular Babe allowed three runs, but the Cardinals went on to win, 9-7.

Got your October total? Here's how it breaks down:

WALK-OFF BOMB TO WIN GAME SEVEN AND MVP HONORS	= 45-50
WON A RING IN A THRILLING SEVEN-GAME SERIES	= 40-44
GOOD JOB – YOU DID ENOUGH TO GET THE RING	= 35-39
LOST A TOUGH SEVEN-GAME SERIES	= 30-34
THEY'RE CALLING YOU THE "NEW" BILL BUCKNER	= 00-29

Think you can do better next season? Well, you're going to get a shot at it – get ready for Boston Red Sox IQ, Volume II!

About the Author

Bill Nowlin has written a couple of dozen books on the Boston Red Sox, including *Red Sox Threads* and *Day by Day with the Boston Red Sox*. He's also edited a number of "team books" on the Red Sox, in collaboration with colleagues from the Society of American Baseball Research (SABR), which he serves as Vice President. Among the SABR books are *The 1967 Impossible Dream Red Sox* and books on the 1918 Sox, the 1939 team, the 1948 team, and the 1975 team. A volume on the 1912 Red Sox is in the works.

Readers are invited to offer suggestions for future Red Sox IQ books, or questions, comments, or corrections to anything in this volume by writing to him at: bnowlin@rounder.com

References

Abrams, Roger, *The First World Series and the Baseball Fanatics of 1903* (Boston: Northeastern University Press, 2003)

Ballou, Bill, *Behind the Green Monster* (Chicago: Triumph Books, 2009)

Burgess, Chuck and Bill Nowlin, *Love That Dirty Water* (Burlington MA: Rounder Books, 2007)

Kaese, Harold, *A Rooter's Guide to the Red Sox* (privately printed, 1974)

Linn, Ed, *Hitter* (NY: Harcourt, Brace, 1993)

Montville, Leigh, *The Big Bam* (NY: Doubleday, 2006)

Montville, Leigh, *Ted Williams* (NY: Doubleday, 2004)

Nowlin, Bill, *Day By Day with the Boston Red Sox* (Burlington MA: Rounder Books, 2007)

Nowlin, Bill, *Mr. Red Sox: The Johnny Pesky Story* (Cambridge: Rounder Books, 2004)

Nowlin, Bill, *Red Sox Threads: Odds and Ends from Red Sox History* (Burlington MA: Rounder Books, 2008)

Nowlin, Bill, *Ted Williams At War* (Burlington MA: Rounder Books, 2007)

Nowlin, Bill and Jim Prime, *The Red Sox World Series Encyclopedia* (Burlington MA: Rounder Books, 2008)

Nowlin, Bill and David Vincent, *The Ultimate Red Sox Home Run Guide* (Burlington MA: Rounder Books, 2009)

Prime, Jim with Bill Nowlin, *Tales from the Red Sox Dugout* (Champaign: Sports Publishing, 2000)

Prime, Jim and Bill Nowlin, *More Tales from the Red Sox Dugout: Yarns from the Sox* (Champaign: Sports Publishing, 2002)

Shaughnessy, Dan, *At Fenway* (NY: Three Rivers, 1996)

Stout, Glenn and Richard Johnson, *Red Sox Century* (Boston: Houghton Mifflin, 2004)

Tan, Cecilia, and Bill Nowlin, *The 50 Greatest Red Sox Games* (NY: John Wiley, 2006)

Thompson, Dick, *The Ferrell Brothers of Baseball* (Jefferson NC: McFarland, 2005)

Thorn, John, Phil Birnbaum, and Bill Deane, *Total Baseball* (Toronto: Sport Classic, 2004)

Walton, Ed, *Red Sox Triumphs and Tragedies* (NY: Stein and Day, 1980)

Walton, Ed, *This Date in Red Sox History* (NY: Scarborough, 1978)

Also by Bill Nowlin

The Boston Red Sox World Series Encyclopedia
by Bill Nowlin and Jim Prime

What a difference a millennium makes! With the "Curse" a distant memory, the Boston Red Sox are the first team this century to win two World Series titles.

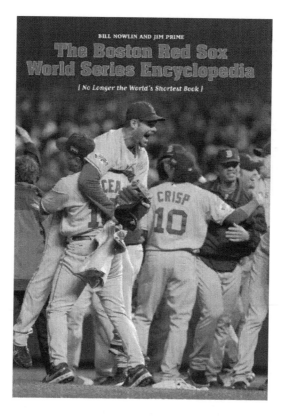

The Red Sox World Series Encyclopedia is the result of another collaboration by veteran Red Sox historians Bill Nowlin and Jim Prime and includes full game accounts of every one of the 67 Series games played (to date) and profiles a significant player from each game.

Richly supplemented with dozens of lists, tables, and stats, the book will provide a solid and eminently readable companion as the team prepares for additional Series in the years to come.

The Ultimate Red Sox Home Run Guide
by Bill Nowlin and David Vincent

Going . . . going . . . gone!

Hitting the ball out of the park is one of the most electrifying acts – and one of the most difficult to accomplish – in sport. The Red Sox have been known as a slugging team for many years, and are one of the few to have hit over 11,000 major league homers.

The Ultimate Red Sox Home Run Guide takes a look Red Sox homers from the regular season to the postseason, with nearly 150 lists, sometimes serious and sometimes light-hearted.

Follow the exploits of Ted Williams and Manny Ramirez, Carl Yastrzemski and David Ortiz, and the great home runs of Carlton Fisk, Tony C, Bill Mueller, and Rico Petrocelli.

Learn about how home runs have changed over the years, and read vignettes highlighting important moments of Red Sox homer history. It's all here – plenty for the scholar and plenty to settle a bet in the barroom.

Lefty, Double-X, and The Kid: The 1939 Red Sox, a Team in Transition
edited by Bill Nowlin

Why 1939? It was Ted Williams' rookie year, and Bobby Doerr's second. Jimmie Foxx was coming off a 50 home run year and the 1938 batting title. Two other Hall of Famers – Lefty Grove and Joe Cronin – helped anchor the team.

It was a year of transition and of hope, emerging from the doldrums that had plagued the Red Sox since 1918 – a stretch that included nine last-place finishes in 16 years, until Tom Yawkey bought the team in 1934 and began to pump money in to prompt a revival.

The team had a slugging Bohemian (Joe Vosmik), a snappy-dressing clothes horse (Broadway Charlie Wagner) and a bonafide espionage agent (Moe Berg), who worked for U.S. intelligence during the Second World War, which was just around the corner.

There were an unusual number of interesting characters on the team, and some 19 Society for American Baseball Research authors and editors have combined to present a picture of one of the more colorful Red Sox teams of years gone by.

Red Sox Threads / Odds & Ends from Red Sox History
by Bill Nowlin

Red Sox Threads is a collection of tangents and tidbits Bill Nowlin assembled while working on a dozen books about the Red Sox.

Spinning the many stories of Red Sox history has led to rich and rewarding finds - the first Latino on the Red Sox (Frank Arellanes, 1908) and the first Native American (Case Patten, also 1908), the best and worst Opening Day and Patriots Day games, players who were stabbed or shot or killed themselves, and those who served in the military.

Learn about the only Red Sox player to play before the President of the US, the King of England, and have an audience with the Pope. Stats and streaks and hidden ball tricks, all the players who homered in their last at-bat, players who filled in as umpires during games, the time the whole team showed up to play in the wrong city, the night two men were killed in the wreck of the train transporting the team . . . think of a thread to follow and there's a good chance it's unraveled here.

When Boston Still Had The Babe / The 1918 World Champion Red Sox
edited by Bill Nowlin

Late into the Boston Red Sox' infamous 86-year championship drought – from 1918 to 2004 – it became nearly taboo to talk seriously about the 1918 team.

In 1919 owner Harry Frazee sold Babe Ruth to the Yankees, who went on to win their first of many titles. Some believed the Red Sox were cursed. The year the Sox had last won it all, 1918, became a sing-song taunt delivered by mocking Yankees fans.

This overlooked season was a fascinating one, played in the shadow of the first World War with dozens of players leaving baseball for military service or war-related work all year long.

Day by Day with the Boston Red Sox by Bill Nowlin

Are you one of those many dedicated fans who can't live without the Red Sox, or do you know someone who is? Or perhaps you're a casual fan seeking to expand your knowledge of Red Sox history through easily-digestible, bite-sized morsels?

For your daily dose of Bosox, look no further than *Day by Day with the Boston Red Sox*. Encompassing every day of the year, this overflowing volume takes the reader through more than a century of Red Sox lore – from the great and glorious victories to the discouraging and depressing defeats. There is the agony, but also the ecstasy. There are the trades and transactions, the debuts, the birth dates and dates of passing of members of the Red Sox past and present, and many more milestones along the way.

Don't confuse this book with medicine, though – while many of the vignettes here will make you feel better, some – be forewarned – may make you sick. Boasting over 6,500 informative nuggets of information, Day by Day with the Boston Red Sox covers all the bases of triumph and tragedy alike, with equal measures of dry wit, comprehensive research, and passionate fandom.

Day by Day with the Boston Red Sox features:
- Nearly 4,000 separate entries documenting a range of subjects: wins, losses, fielding feats, hitting achievements, statistical anomalies, personal quirks, and much more!
- Over 1,000 player trades and transactions!
- Birthdays and Red Sox debut dates of over 1,500 players past and present – information which is also

collected in a handy alphabetical appendix for quick reference!

Ted Williams at War
by Bill Nowlin

"He did a helluva good job. Ted only batted .406 for the Red Sox. He batted a thousand for the Marine Corps and the United States." - John Glenn, U.S. Senator and former astronaut

Ted Williams was the only Hall of Fame ballplayer who saw military service in two wars. He was a flight instructor with the United States Marine Corps in World War II and flew 39 combat missions in the Korean War - several of them as wingman for squadron mate John Glenn. Shot down once, on his third mission, Williams was lucky to escape with his life. He was back up and flying less than 24 hours later.

There aren't too many athletes who are truly heroes. Ted Williams was one such athlete. Imagine Alex Rodriguez or Barry Bonds flying dive-bombing missions in close air support of troops on the ground, taking anti-aircraft fire as they pulled out of dives as low as 500 feet. Imagine the records Williams might have set had he not devoted nearly five full seasons to serving his country.

Most biographies of Ted Williams devote a chapter or two to the five years he spent in the Marines. Bill Nowlin has interviewed over 40 pilots who flew with Capt. Williams from K-3 in Korea, and interviewed over 120 people in all who knew or encountered Ted Williams during his years of service. Combined with access to Williams' squadron records, his personal flight logbooks, and his fitness and evaluation reports, Ted Williams At War presents by far the most comprehensive portrait of a man that many termed "the real John Wayne."

Features a wealth of over 100 photographs (most previously unpublished) from Ted's time in the service.

The Kid: Ted Williams in San Diego
edited by Bill Nowlin

The years before Ted Williams came to Boston were the formative years that created The Kid and shaped the Splendid Splinter. He was lucky to have grown up in San Diego, he often said, where a kid can play baseball year-round. At the same time he recognized that had he been seen as Hispanic (his maternal grandparents were both Mexican), he would have suffered from the prejudices of the day. A high school hero and a solid player for two seasons with his hometown San Diego Padres, Ted Williams came from a remarkable family – his mother a Salvation Army evangelist and his father a photographer, and uncles who were cowboys, longshoremen, cement truck drivers, mariachi musicians, and ballplayers. Nine members of the Society for American Baseball Research contribute detailed accounts of Ted's sandlot games, his high school career, his two years with the Padres, and even his year in Minneapolis before becoming Boston's best ballplayer – and very possibly the greatest hitter who ever lived.

Inevitably, Williams biographies spend only a chapter or two on his early years. This book focuses entirely on the first twenty years of Ted's life – the years before he joined the Boston Red Sox and broke onto the national scene by setting a rookie RBI record (145 runs batted in) that has never been beaten. These are the years that forged the future baseball star, and the man who became a world class sport fisherman, and the man who flew wing for John Glenn in the F-9F Panther jet in numerous dive-bombing missions during the Korean War.

Spahn, Sain and Teddy Ballgame: Boston's (almost) Perfect Baseball Summer of 1948
Edited by Bill Nowlin

In 1948, the Boston Braves won the National League pennant and went to the World Series. The Red Sox and the Cleveland Indians were tied at the end of the season; the Sox lost a one-game playoff. That one loss prevented a Braves/Red Sox Fall Classic in which the two teams located within a mile of each other would have played for the baseball championship of the world.

It was a terrific summer of baseball featuring names that still evoke one of the golden eras of baseball - Warren Spahn, Johnny Sain, and Ted Williams, and favorites like Dom DiMaggio, Mel Parnell, Tommy Holmes, Sibby Sisti.

The 1967 Impossible Dream Red Sox: Pandemonium On The Field
edited by Bill Nowlin and Dan Desrochers

When Jim Lonborg induced Minnesota's Rich Rollins to pop up, and shortstop Rico Petrocelli stepped back and cradled the softly-looped fly ball, the '67 Sox had done the impossible – they had overcome 100-to-1 odds, climbing out of ninth place the year before to capture the American League pennant. It had been 21 years since the Sox last reached the post-season.

Dozens, then hundreds, then thousands of fans streamed out onto the Fenway infield mobbing Lonborg, who lost a shirt and his shoelaces as he struggled through the delirious crowd to get to the clubhouse. Two or three dozen fans climbed the backstop screen toward the broadcast booth. Others dismantled the scoreboard in left field. Many just tore out handfuls of grass and stuffed their pockets. It truly was, in the words of Red Sox radio announcer Ned Martin, "pandemonium on the field."

As Peter Gammons once wrote on this great season, "The Red Sox were always New England's team, yes, but it took the Impossible Dream of 1967 to turn it into a romanticized mystique and keep the legion of fans coming by the millions . . . It wasn't always the way it is now, and might never have been but for '67."

Mr. Red Sox - The Johnny Pesky Story
by Bill Nowlin

With a baseball career spanning eight decades, Johnny has been clubhouse kid, major league shortstop (with stats better than several Hall of Famers), coach, manager, broadcaster and a special evaluator of talent.

This is the first biography of Pesky ever published, and also includes a foreword by Ted Williams, unique photos from Pesky's own collection, and rare images from other sources.

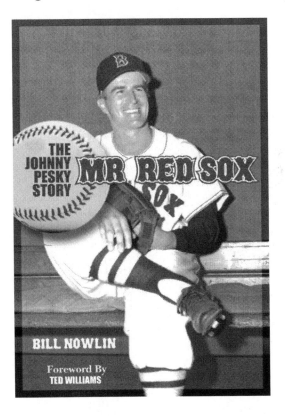

Sports by the Numbers

The award-winning Sports by the Numbers book series is a proud sponsor of Black Mesa's IQ books. SBTN is the series where every number tells a story – and whether you're a beginning fan just learning the ropes, or a diehard fanatic hanging on the outcome of every game, the crew at SBTN have got you covered.

Check out Sports by the Numbers on the web:

www.sportsbythenumbers.com

Current titles include:

- *University of Oklahoma Football*
- *University of Georgia Football*
- *Penn State University Football*
- *Major League Baseball*
- *New York Yankees*
- *Mixed Martial Arts*
- *NASCAR*
- *Sacramento Kings Basketball*

For information about special discounts for bulk purchases, please email: sales@savasbeatie.com

Sports by the Numbers Praise

"You think you know it all? Not so fast. To unearth fact upon fact about this historic franchise in a unique yet tangible way is an impressive feat, which is why the following pages are more than worthwhile for every member of that cult known as Red Sox Nation . . . This is a book that Red Sox fans of all ages and types will enjoy and absorb."
   — Ian Browne, Boston Red Sox Beat Writer,
   MLB.com

"Fighting is physical storytelling where villains and heroes emerge, but the back-story is what makes the sport something that persisted from B.C. times to what we know it as today. Antonio Rodrigo Nogueira living through a childhood coma only to demonstrate equal grit inside the ring on his way to two world championships. Randy Couture defying age like it was as natural as sunrise on his way to six world championships. The achievements are endless in nature, but thanks to this book, these great human narratives are translated into a universal language—numbers—in a universal medium—fighting."
   — Danny Acosta, Sherdog.com and *Fight!* Magazine
   Writer

"Statistics have long been resigned to slower, contemplative sports. Finally, they get a crack at the world's fastest sport in this fascinating piece of MMA analysis."
   — Ben Zeidler, CagePotato.com, *Fight!* Magazine

"Long-time Sooner fans will revel in the flood of memories that flow from these pages. You'll think back to a defining moment—that favorite player, an afternoon next to the radio, or that special day at Owen Field. And the information contained here is so thorough that you'll relive those memories many times."
 — Bob Stoops, Head Coach, University of Oklahoma Football

"*University of Oklahoma Football – S*ports By The Numbers is a must read for all OU Football junkies. I read trivia I didn't know or had forgotten."
 — Barry Switzer, Legendary Head Coach, University of Oklahoma Football

"Clever and insightful. For fans who don't know much about the history of stock-car racing, it's like taking the green flag."
 — Monte Dutton, best-selling NASCAR author

"This book is fascinating and informative. If you love Yankees trivia, this is the reference for you."
 — Jane Heller, best-selling novelist, Yankees blogger, and author of *Confessions of a She-Fan: The Course of True Love with the New York Yankees*

"This book brings you tons of info on America's best loved and most hated team—the New York Yankees . . . a great book for any age or fan of America's Game and Team. A must read."
 — Phil Speranza, author of the *2000 Yankee Encyclopedia 5th edition*

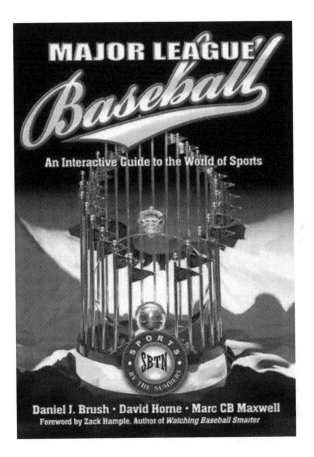

"You will find the most important numbers that every fan should know, like Joe DiMaggio's 56-game hitting streak, Ted Williams' .406 batting average, Hank Aaron's 755 homeruns, and Nolan Ryan's seven no-hitters, but there are hundreds of lesser-known stats. Even if you think you know everything about baseball, I guarantee you will learn a whole lot from this book."
— Zack Hample, best-selling author of *Watching Baseball Smarter*

"I loved this book. I could not put it down at night. This book is the perfect bedside or coffee table reading material. *New York Yankees: An Interactive Guide to the World of Sports* has a huge collection of interesting data about the entire New York Yankees history."
    — Sam Hendricks, author of *Fantasy Football Guidebook* and *Fantasy Football Almanac 2009*

"The Yankees matter—but you already knew that, and soon, you will dive into this wonderful yield by the good folks at Sports by the Numbers and you will lose yourself in baseball, in history, in numbers, and in the New York Yankees. I envy you. I can't think of a better way to pass the next couple of hours."
    — Mike Vaccaro, best-selling author and award-winning columnist for the *New York Post*

Black Mesa Titles

Look for these other titles in the IQ Series:

- *Mixed Martial Arts*
- *Atlanta Braves*
- *New York Yankees*
- *Cincinnati Reds*
- *Milwaukee Brewers*
- *St. Louis Cardinals*
- *University of Oklahoma Football*
- *University of Georgia Football*
- *University of Florida Football*
- *Penn State Football*
- *Boston Celtics*

Look for your favorite MLB and collegiate teams in Black Mesa's *If I was the Bat Boy* series, and look for your favorite NFL and collegiate teams in Black Mesa's *How to Build the Perfect Player* series, both by award-winning artist and author Cameron Silver.

For information about special discounts for bulk purchases, please email:
black.mesa.publishing@gmail.com

Praise for MMA IQ

"Every time I work on a cut I am being tested and I feel confident I can pass the test. After reading MMA IQ I'm not so sure I can do the same with this book."
— UFC Cutman Jacob "Stitch" Duran,
www.stitchdurangear.com

"MMA fans everywhere pay attention—this is your best chance to reign supreme in your favorite bar stool. The trivia and stories come at you so fast and so furious you'll wish Stitch Duran was in your corner getting you ready to do battle."
— Sam Hendricks, award-winning author of
Fantasy Football Tips: 201 Ways to Win through Player Rankings, Cheat Sheets and Better Drafting

"From the rookie fan to the pound for pound trivia champs, MMA IQ has something that will challenge the wide spectrum of fans that follow the sport."
— Robert Joyner, www.mmapayout.com

"I thought I knew MMA, but this book took my MMA IQ to a whole new level . . . fun read, highly recommended."
— William Li, www.findmmagym.com

You can visit Mixed Martial Arts IQ author Zac Robinson on the web:

www.sportsbythenumbersmma.com
www.cutmanstitchduran.com

Praise for NY Yankees IQ

"If you consider yourself a tested veteran at baseball trivia in general or a hardcore expert at Yankees trivia in particular, it doesn't matter—you owe it to yourself to test your skills with this IQ book, because only when you pass this test can you truly claim to be a cut above everyone else."

> — Daniel J. Brush, award-winning author of *New York Yankees: An Interactive Guide to the World of Sports*

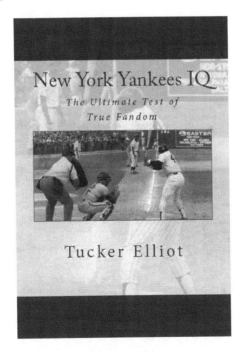

Praise for Atlanta Braves IQ

"There are just two Hall of Famers who really know the Braves road from Boston to Milwaukee to Atlanta—Eddie Mathews and Braves IQ! This book will determine if you can win fourteen-straight division titles or if you will get lost trying to get off I-285. If you're a Braves fan or you know a Braves fan, this is a must-have."

— Dr. Keith Gaddie, award-winning broadcast journalist and author of *University of Georgia Football: An Interactive Guide to the World of Sports*

Made in the USA
Middletown, DE
15 December 2017